THE BRITISH INSTITUTE OF INTERNATIONAL AND COMPARATIVE LAW
and
THE BRITISH INSTITUTE OF HUMAN RIGHTS

ASPECTS OF INCORPORATION OF THE EUROPEAN CONVENTION OF HUMAN RIGHTS INTO DOMESTIC LAW

1993

The present volume is respectfully
dedicated to the memory of
Sir James Fawcett DSC, QC
Member of the European Commission
of Human Rights for 22 years
and its President from 1972 to 1982

The British Institute of International and Comparative Law

and

The British Institute of Human Rights

Published by
The British Institute of International and Comparative Law
and
The British Institute of Human Rights

British Library Cataloguing in Publication Data

Aspects of Incorporation of the European
Convention of Human Rights into Domestic
Law

I. Gardner, J. P.
341.481

ISBN 0 903067 38 2

Printed in Great Britain by Bourne Press Limited

Distributed by
The British Institute of International and Comparative Law
Charles Clore House, 17 Russell Square, London WC1B 5DR
and
The British Institute of Human Rights
King's College, Strand, London WC2R 2LS

FOREWORD

The Rt. Hon. Lord Scarman OBE
President of the British Institute of Human Rights

THE European Convention on Human Rights and Fundamental Freedoms was signed in 1950 and came into force in 1953. It is based on the Universal Declaration of Human Rights proclaimed by the General Assembly of the United Nations on 10 December 1948. The Convention was prepared by the Council of Europe: its aim was, and remains, to protect and enforce the human rights upon which depend the fundamental freedoms "which are the foundation of justice and peace in the world".

Most European countries are parties to the Convention: they are Austria, Belgium, Bulgaria, Czech and Slovak Republic, Cyprus, Denmark, Estonia*, Finland, France, Germany, Greece, Hungary, Iceland, Ireland, Italy, Liechtenstein, Lithuania*, Luxembourg, Malta, Netherlands, Norway, Poland, Portugal, San Marino, Slovenia*, Spain, Sweden, Switzerland, Turkey and the United Kingdom.

The jurisprudence of the European Community as developed by the Court of Justice of the Community recognises the Convention as the standard-setter in cases in which the Court has to consider and decide a human rights issue. The great majority of the signatory States have in one way or another incorporated the declaratory provisions of the Convention into their domestic law, this being the straightforward way of ensuring an effective protection and enforcement of the human rights which the Convention by Article 1 requires that 'the High Contracting Parties shall secure to everyone within their jurisdiction'.

The United Kingdom has not incorporated the declaratory provisions of the Convention into its domestic law. Why not? It has accepted as a State the obligations of the Convention. But we have a domestic system of laws into which our internationally accepted obligations do not intrude unless embodied in an Act of Parliament. Why doesn't Parliament pass legislation protecting and rendering enforceable in our national courts the rights and freedoms of the Convention which as a State it is our duty to secure to everyone within the Kingdom?

Perhaps we are too proud. In the past we as a nation have been pleased from time to time to legislate to protect the civil rights and liberties of our people. The

* Signed but not yet ratified the Convention.

Magna Carta, extracted from King John in 1215, was later made a statute; the settlement of 1688 which we invited the co-operative William, Prince of Orange,to accept as the terms upon which he and Mary succeeded the Stuarts, became an Act of Parliament; and there have been many other statutes over the centuries to protect the liberties of the individual, notably the habeas corpus legislation. Historically, our freedoms have enjoyed the protection of the common law, supplemented by statute for more than 700 years.

Did we need to reform our law in 1950? The Government answered this question then with a resounding 'No need'. Can we be so sure now?

However, this remains the official stance today. The view has been and remains that any little hiccough between our domestic law and our international obligations under the Convention can be remedied by *ad hoc* administrative or legislative action after the defect or omission in our existing law has been made apparent. In 1991 we can see that this view is absurdly complacent and is responsible for major injustice. The gaps between our law and our Convention obligations have been shown by a long series of decisions in the European Court of Human Rights to be too serious, too great, and too numerous for minor mending after the hole in the garment of the law has become evident. Moreover, the injustices suffered by those of our people whose human rights have been infringed, who could find no relief or remedy in our own courts, and who have had to persevere in their pursuit of right all the way to Strasbourg after 'exhausting their remedies' at home, are a scandal and mock our reputation as a country where the rights of everyone are respected and, if need be, effectively enforced.

The papers revised since the Conference on the implications of incorporation of the Convention into domestic law should prove valuable. We are glad that we had with us Judge Ryssdal, President of the European Court of Human Rights, and Professor Nørgaard, President of the European Commission of Human Rights, with some of their colleagues. It is good, too, that some of our senior judges participated. We shall surely hear of the disarray which is currently emerging in our senior appellate courts when a question arises of human rights protected by the Convention for consideration and decision. Some appeal judges - not enough of them in my opinion - face the Convention, read it, and covertly but sensibly apply it. Others will have nothing to do with it but slyly move our internal law in its direction. Some (mercifully a minority) regard the Convention as at best an international obligation with which our law, if it be ambiguous, can be interpreted so as to harmonise. But none ignore it.

Let's be done with this legal wriggling and these subtle confusions. Let us enact the declaratory provisions of the Convention. We shall then have a body of statute law which our judges can apply in their usual way, according to well-understood principles. And our people will have what today they lack - courts at home to which the oppressed and the aggrieved citizen can go and get his human right vindicated, protected and enforced without prolonged delay, expense and frustration.

TABLE OF CONTENTS

PREFACE

THE present volume arises from papers given at a Conference organised jointly by the British Institute of Human Rights and the British Institute of International and Comparative Law, held in May 1991 on *Aspects of Incorporation of the European Human Rights Convention into Domestic Law*.

The purpose of the Conference was threefold: first, to examine the content of the obligations which the Convention itself imposes and the way in which the case-law of the European Commission and Court of Human Rights in Strasbourg reflects the practice of Member States of the Council of Europe which have and have not incorporated the Convention into their domestic law; secondly, to examine the approach to incorporation in some of the other Member States of the Council of Europe; and, thirdly, to review the treatment of the Convention in English domestic law and the responses which the United Kingdom has made to the particular requirements of the Convention.

The object of the Conference was not therefore to advocate incorporation of the Convention into the domestic law of the United Kingdom, although many advocates of this course were among the practitioners, judges, government legal advisers and academics who participated in the Conference, the final session of which included a discussion of specific proposals for incorporation. The participants at the Conference who delivered papers or chaired sessions included, in addition to those whose papers are published here, Lord Browne-Wilkinson, Sir Basil Hall, Professor Rosalyn Higgins QC, Anthony Lester QC and Clive Nicholls QC.

The present collection of papers, which have been revised for publication, do not include that discussion and concentrate on the neutral examination of the legal issues to which incorporation and non-incorporation respectively give rise. The papers are therefore divided into three sections: first, the requirements of the Convention; secondly, a review of some national approaches to incorporation of the Convention into domestic law; and, thirdly, an analysis of the Convention's place in the laws of the United Kingdom.

Professor Frowein's paper provides a very clear introduction to some of the particular difficulties arising from the interpretation of the Convention and the differing legal regimes relating to its application in domestic law. He deals in particular with the apparently clear terms of Article 13 of the Convention and the contrast between that text and the practice of States applying a dualist system of the reception of public international law into domestic law. He refers here to the attitude of the Scandinavian countries, the United Kingdom and Ireland, to the incorporation of the Convention and explores the question whether the change in practice amongst the majority of Member States of the Council of Europe, including the changes referred to in this volume by Judge Ryssdal and Professor Nørgaard in Norway and Denmark respectively, could justify a reassessment of whether the Convention imposes an obligation to incorporate. The subsequent increase in the number of Member States of the Council of Europe and their generalised acceptance of the Convention in their domestic laws provide a major reason why the issues discussed here are as topical now as when the initial Conference was held.

In the second part of his paper, Professor Frowein describes the place of the Convention in German law in particular in the light of the wide-ranging constitutional guarantees provided by the Basic Law. This survey reveals, first, that notwithstanding the scope of the guarantees in the Basic Law to which the domestic courts are bound to refer in preference to the provisions of the Convention, specific guarantees in the Convention which are not reflected expressly in the Basic Law have been relied upon in major judicial decisions and there are some signs that the highest courts are becoming more prepared to refer to the provisions of the Convention. Secondly the inevitable possibility of a further 'appeal' from a decision of the Federal Constitutional Court to the European control mechanisms in Strasbourg is naturally not excluded by the existence of an individual constitutional remedy and the application of the Convention in domestic law. This raises a theme developed elsewhere in the volume of the effect of judgments of the European Court of Human Rights on previous judgments of the domestic courts and reveals a distinction between incorporation of the legal rules in Part I of the Convention and incorporation of procedural mechanisms for the implementation of the Convention's interpretation.

These themes are also reflected in Dr. Krüger's paper on the effect of incorporation on the type and scale of cases examined by the Commission and the Court. This review emphasises that a consideration of aspects of incorporation must include a review of the way in which incorporation is achieved in different legal systems. The varied constitutional traditions of the Member States of the Council of Europe imply that there is no one form of incorporation and the particular method of incorporation chosen by a given State has important repercussions for the rule requiring the exhaustion of domestic remedies. Dr. Krüger's analysis of this issue underlines the fundamental procedural differences between domestic proceedings and applications to the Commission and to the Court. These are particularly highlighted by the comparative informality of the pleading in applications under Article 25 of the Convention when compared with the rigorous requirements of the domestic courts in this respect. Although the Commission has traditionally applied a fairly generous interpretation of the requirement to raise a Convention argument 'at least in substance' before the domestic authorities, Dr. Krüger's emphasis on the importance of requiring applicants to pursue domestic remedies where their outcome is merely doubtful reflects the subsidiary role of the Convention machinery. The primary responsibility for the protection of fundamental rights lies with the national jurisdiction.

This section of the chapter also reviews the significance of constitutional challenges to legislation, an aspect of the Convention's jurisdiction which is the subject of my own contribution in Chapter 8. It is perhaps significant that the Commission's interpretation of Article 26 of the Convention, whereby individuals are not required to seek 'incidental constitutional review' of the conformity of the legislation with the national constitution, effectively facilitates challenges of legislation before the Commission and the Court for conformity with the Convention.

The final part of Dr. Krüger's chapter reviews the statistical implications of incorporation on the number of applications lodged with the Commission and the Court. Since the opportunity of lodging an application under Article 25 remains where the Convention has been incorporated although it will obviously only be exercised by litigants who have failed in the domestic jurisdiction, the statistics seem to suggest that the total number of applications against a particular Member State is not significantly affected by incorporation, although the nature of the complaints may well be.

The second section of the volume contains three chapters illustrating some national approaches to the place of the Convention in domestic law and to proposals for its incorporation. The selection of the jurisdictions concerned, Norway, Denmark and the United Kingdom, arose not only because of the fortuitous combination in the Presidents of the European Court and Commission of Human Rights of Judge Ryssdal and Professor Nørgaard respectively but from the important similarities between the approach of these two Scandinavian jurisdictions to the place of the Convention in their domestic law to the position in the United Kingdom. Both countries recognise a dualist conception of international law similar to that adopted by the United Kingdom. As a result, international treaties may be incorporated into domestic law by a specific legislative enactment but their status, if not so incorporated, is as an aid to the construction and interpretation of domestic law. As a result, the influence of the Convention in Norway, Denmark and in the United Kingdom is very largely one for the courts to explain on a case-by-case basis.

A further result of these features is that several aspects of the practice as described by Judge Ryssdal and Professor Nørgaard in Norway and Denmark respectively bear considerable similarity to aspects of the position of the Convention in the law of the United Kingdom described by Nicolas Bratza QC in Chapter 6. This is true of the basic premise of Norwegian law that the Convention is binding on but not in Norway and to the uncertain position of the Convention which Professor Nørgaard describes in Danish law prior to 1 July 1992 when the Convention became incorporated into Danish law.

In the light of the discussion and the development of the place of the Convention in English law, the progressive development of its interpretation by both the Norwegian and the Danish courts is of particular interest. Judge Ryssdal describes the principal of presumption in the interpretation of Norwegian law that the Norwegian courts should prefer an interpretation and development of the law which reflects the international obligations assumed by Norway. This procedure is in part familiar to English lawyers and shows a progressive approach to the incorporation of the Convention. As Judge Ryssdal explains, this is true not only in the development of the interpretation of case law by the Supreme Court of Norway but also through the progessive adoption of legislation extending the operation of the Convention to different areas of Norwegian law starting with the Code of Criminal Procedure and thereafter extending its direct application to the interpretation of the Code of Civil Procedure. Perhaps as a result, a major feature of the debate on incorporation of the Convention as a whole into Norwegian law, which culminated with the publication of the Governmental Report recommending its incorporation adopted on 28 May 1993, has dealt with the appropriate status which the Convention should be given within the Norwegian legal hierarchy. As the present volume is prepared for the press, this question remains to be resolved.

Some clues to its possible resolution and illustrations of practical solutions to the issues of incorporating the Convention into a dualist jurisdiction are given by Professor Nørgaard in Chapter 4. He describes some of the features which were identified by the Expert Committee which examined the question of incorporation of the Convention into Danish law as giving rise to particular difficulty, many of which are familiar to common lawyers who have examined the question from the point of view of the United Kingdom. The first familiar feature is the primacy of the legislature in ensuring Danish compliance with the Convention. Professor Nørgaard describes the scrutiny which is given by the Danish Parliament to judgments of the Court, whether relating to Denmark or not, which allow the legislature to ensure that the conformity of Danish law with the Convention is kept under review whenever necessary. This emphasis on the primary role of the legislature is particularly reflected in Professor Nørgaard's summary of key aspects of the debate on incorporation of the Convention into Danish law. This example suggests that further consideration might be given in the United Kingdom to a particular role for Parliament in continuing to ensure compliance with the Convention, even if it were to be incorporated into United Kingdom law.

In the final paragraph of this section, Robert Blackburn reviews legislative proposals which have been made to incorporate the Convention into United Kingdom domestic law. He reviews the legislative history of specific proposals originating from the mid-1970s which have gradually evolved to provide a series of well-structured and fully drafted proposals for incorporation should the political will for this step be present. Robert Blackburn highlights the distinction between the incorporation of the Convention in domestic law and the adoption of an entrenched bill of rights and illustrates the issues raised by Dr. Krüger in Chapter 2 as to the various methods of incorporation which may be adopted to reflect differing constitutional traditions. The approach described here draws upon the experience of the European Communities Act 1972 to entrench a presumption that Parliament does not intend in subsequent legislation to cut down on the guarantees of the Convention.

The final section consists of four chapters dealing with different aspects of the place of the Convention in the law of the United Kingdom. The first of these is a review by Nicolas Bratza QC of the treatment and interpretation of the Convention by the English courts. The difficulty of ascribing a clear place to the position of the Convention in English law recalls in particular aspects of Danish law described by Professor Nørgaard in Chapter 4. Despite the comparative frequency of cases which refer to the Convention, careful analysis reveals that the Convention has seldom been decisive or expressed to be decisive in reaching the final outcome. Two notable features emerge from this review. First, the comparatively frequent references by English judges to the prospects of a particular litigant having to or having the opportunity to pursue their complaint further in Strasbourg coupled at times with an implicit assumption that the outcome of such an application may ultimately vindicate their rights. This factor goes some way to answer those critics who doubt the ability of the English judiciary to interpret the Convention if it was their task.

A second feature has been the concentration of cases in which the Convention has been referred to and even relied upon in cases relating to freedom of expression. Nicolas Bratza deals here with the unpredictable consequences of the judgment of the House of Lords in *Brind* as an example both of particular reliance on the Convention in freedom of expression cases and on the remaining uncertainties as to the extent to which the Convention can be pleaded to establish as well as to resolve an ambiguity in the interpretation of a statute.

Both these issues have been the subject of further major cases since this Chapter was prepared, notably including *Derbyshire County Council v. Times Newspapers*[1] and *Rantzen v. Mirror Group Newspapers and Others*.[2]

The *Derbyshire* case concerned as a preliminary issue whether a county council could sue for libel, a point on which there was (in the view of the Court of Appeal) conflicting first instance authority. The recognition of such a right was challenged by the defendants in those proceedings on the grounds that it would be contrary to Article 10 of the Convention which protects the right to freedom of expression. It was held at first instance that the local authority could sue for libel but this conclusion was reversed by the Court of Appeal in terms which placed extensive reliance upon Article 10 of the Convention. Lords Justices Balcombe and Butler-Sloss in particular had recourse to the Convention because they found the state of the common law on the question before the Court to be uncertain and the Convention to be relevant to its resolution. In concluding that the local authority had no action in defamation, the Court rejected the view that Article 10 required a balance to be struck between the freedom of expression of the newspapers whose article was impugned in the intended libel action and the claim to reputation which the local authority would assert. Article 10 was relied on instead as a reason for not interpreting a common law right for the local authority to sue for damages unless the interference which the creation of such a right would represent with freedom of expression in general could be justified under the terms of Article 10, paragraph 2. In accepting this analysis, the Court of Appeal seemed to view its own role almost as that of legislator in an area of legal uncertainty rather than as a court faced with deciding the issue in the particular case before it.

1. [1992] 3 All ER 65 (CA), [993] 1 All ER 1011 (HL).
2. The *Times* 6 April 1993 (CA).

The House of Lords in a single judgment of Lord Keith concluded that the County Council had no right to sue for damages. The final words of his speech are perhaps worth quoting in the light of the reference made to the judgment of the Court of Appeal above

> My Lords, I have reached my conclusion upon the common law of England without finding any need to rely upon the European Convention. Lord Goff of Chieveley in *A-G v Guardian Newspapers Ltd (No 2)* [1988] 3 All ER 545 at 660, [1990] 1 AC 109 at 283-284 expressed the opinion that in the field of freedom of speech there was no difference in principle between English law on the subject and Art 10 of the Convention. I agree, and can only add that I find it satisfactory to be able to conclude that the common law of England is consistent with the obligations assumed by the Crown under the treaty in this particular field.

In the subsequent libel case of *Rantzen v Mirror Group Newspapers* the Court of Appeal relied significantly on Article 10 of the Convention in deciding under section 8 of the Courts and Legal Services Act 1990 and section 8 of Order 59, rule 11(4) RSC whether libel damages were excessive. Relying upon *A-G v Guardian Newspapers Ltd (No. 2)* and *Derbyshire County Council v Times Newspapers Ltd* the Court of Appeal found support for the proposition that Article 10 had a wider role than resolving ambiguity in the interpretation of a statute and could properly be regarded as an articulation of some of the principles underlying the common law. In concluding that it was appropriate for the Court to intervene and reduce the damages awarded in the particular case, the Court of Appeal considered whether the absence of guidelines as to the appropriate level of damages for a jury to award might conflict with the principle enshrined in Article 10 of the Convention that restrictions on the exercise of freedom of expression should be prescribed by law.

It is no easier in the light of these recent cases for a consistent view of the place of the Convention in English law to be formulated now than when the original Conference on this topic was held. The difficulty is illustrated by the coverage in Chapter 7 by Françoise Hampson of the development of the law relating to children in the care of a local authority in England and Wales, particularly in the light of the judgments in the five so-called *Alphabet* cases. Those cases, together with the *Olsson* case contributed to a substantial extension of the content of the right to respect for family life under Article 8 of the Convention and in particular the extent to which the rights of parents are to be regarded as entrenched *vis-à-vis* their own natural children.

The early case law interpreting the Convention in this respect is largely that of the Commission examining cases on admissibility including those between disputing parents by reference to the principle of the best interests of the child. As Françoise Hampson illustrates, the development of the specific rights of parents *vis-à-vis* their children where those children are in the care of the local authority gives rise to issues not only under Article 8 of the Convention but also as to the parents' access to court protected by Article 6 of the Convention to have their claims to access and parental rights over the children determined.

The final two chapters deal with different aspects of the place of the Convention in domestic law. My own contribution concentrates on two related difficulties to which incorporation gives rise and which largely remain to be resolved in the relations between national courts and the Commission and Court of Human Rights both in the United Kingdom and elsewhere. The first of these is the jurisdiction exercised by the Commission and the Court to review legislation for conformity with the Convention. This jurisdiction raises particular problems of *locus standi* and of the consequential effects of review which are in part illustrated by the judgment of the Court of Appeal in the *Derbyshire County Council* case referred to above. Because the Court was asked to consider the availability of an action for defamation as a preliminary issue, the Court of Appeal had to examine the conformity of English law with the Convention. This may be contrasted with the question in *Rantzen v Mirror Group Newspapers Ltd* where a direct application of Article 10 might have raised the question whether the interference with the right to freedom of expression which an excessive award of damages represented was proportionate to the aim sought to be achieved.

The second issue is the interaction of proceedings in the domestic courts and in Strasbourg. Once again the position in European Community law is relevant as an example which could be emulated. A possible development of English law would be to apply domestic interim measures where the conformity of legislation with the Convention is examined by the Commission and the Court.

Robin Churchill in the final chapter deals with the practical question of compliance with the Convention given that it is not incorporated into the law of the United Kingdom by reviewing the effect given to judgments of the Court and decisions of the Committee of Ministers in cases in which violations have been found against the United Kingdom. The survey underlines the particular difficulty to which compliance with the obligations of the Convention without its incorporation into domestic law gives rise. Because the Convention sets an evolving standard, its requirements are not static and compliance requires a regular review of the state of domestic law to ensure that changes in the interpretation of the Convention are properly reflected in national practice. This control can be effectively exercised by the legislature (the situation in Denmark which Professor Nørgaard describes) but the risk of non-compliance must be heightened if the legislature does not keep the development of the interpretation of the Convention under review and if the courts are not able to reflect its requirements because it is not incorporated into domestic law.

It is hoped that this collection may provide the basis for further study of the issues arising from the incorporation and non-incorporation of the European Convention on Human Rights into domestic law. Although the political attitude to incorporation is substantially unchanged since the Conference was held from which these papers derive, the legal debate on the place of the Convention in the law of the United Kingdom and its importance as a cohesive factor in the creation of Europe after the Central European Revolution of 1989 is undiminished.

The thanks of the British Institute of International and Comparative Law and the British Institute of Human Rights are due to all those who have contributed to the preparation and publication of this volume.

J.P. Gardner
London, 1993

NOTE ON CONTRIBUTORS

Robert Blackburn	Deputy Director, The British Institute of Human Rights. Senior Lecturer in Law, King's College, London
Nicolas Bratza, QC	Barrister, Vice-Chairman, The British Institute of Human Rights
R.R. Churchill	Senior Lecturer, Cardiff Law School
J.A. Frowein	Vice President, European Commission of Human Rights, Strasbourg. Director Max Planck Institute for Comparative Public Law and International Law
J.P. Gardner	Director, The British Institute of International and Comparative Law
Françoise Hampson	Senior Lecturer in Law and Human Rights Centre, University of Essex and a Governor of the British Institute of Human Rights
H.C. Krüger	Secretary, European Commission of Human Rights, Strasbourg
C.A. Nørgaard	President, European Commission of Human Rights, Strasbourg
Judge Rolv Ryssdal	President, European Court of Human Rights, Strasbourg

SECTION I:

THE REQUIREMENTS OF THE CONVENTION

Chapter 1

INCORPORATION OF THE CONVENTION INTO DOMESTIC LAW

J.A. Frowein

I. THE CONVENTION AND THE PRINCIPLE OF INCORPORATION

THE Convention is a treaty concluded under the rules of international law and thus primarily creating obligations as between the different member States. The machinery of collective enforcement through the Convention organs on the basis of individual or State applications is the peculiar feature of the European Convention on Human Rights.

The Commission has recently emphasised 'the character of the Convention, as a constitutional instrument of European public order in the field of human rights'.[1] As far back as 1960 in the famous case *Austria v. Italy* the Commission held that it was the purpose of the High Contracting Parties 'to establish a common public order of the free democracies of Europe' and that the obligations undertaken by the parties 'are essentially of an objective character'.[2]

The Court has held that the Convention 'creates, over and above a network of mutual, bilateral undertakings, objective obligations which, in the words of the preamble, benefit from a collective enforcement'.[3]

Article 1 of the Convention makes it clear that the rights guaranteed to individuals under the treaty are individual rights created by public international

1. Decision of 4 March 1991 *Chrysostomos and others v. Turkey, Human Rights Law Journal*, 1991, pp.113,121.
2. *Austria v. Italy, Yearbook of the European Convention on Human Rights*, Vol.4, pp.116,140.
3. Case of *Ireland v. United Kingdom*, Judgment of 18 January 1978, ECHR Series A, Vol.25, p.90.

law. The wording in Article 1 'shall secure' = 'reconnaissent' as opposed to the earlier draft shows that these rights are created by the ratification of the Convention and must be respected by the State immediately without any additional act of implementation.[4]

It is a different matter, however, whether the Convention creates an obligation under public international law to make it as such internally applicable in the municipal law of member States. Such an obligation may well be created by a treaty under public international law as the treaties establishing the European Community, as the most important example, shows.

If one looks at Articles 1 and 13 of the Convention one would at first sight be inclined to accept that the Convention must be made internally applicable. How can a State secure the rights and freedoms 'defined' in Section 1 of the Convention to all individuals without really making these defined rights, with the wording of the definition, as such applicable? Anyone not informed about the specific traditions of States applying the so-called dualist system would certainly come to the conclusion that Article 1 of the Convention presupposes internal applicability of the Convention in municipal law, before administrative organs and courts in all Convention countries.

Article 13 seems to support such an argument. How can a State create an effective remedy before a national authority for those whose rights and freedoms are violated without making it possible to claim the violation of the rights defined in the Convention before that organ? It is no surprise, therefore, that very highly regarded scholars and practitioners have argued for such an obligation from the very beginning.

For instance Professor and Judge Thomas Buergenthal already in the early years of the European Convention on Human Rights took the view that it must contain an obligation to make it internally applicable.[5] In more recent times the same position has been taken by Judge Pescatore with his great experience in the law of European integration.[6] And who could doubt that only incorporation

4. The earlier draft had stated 'undertake to secure', ECHR Series A Vol.25, p.91.

5. T. Buergenthal, 'The Effect of the European Convention on Human Rights on the Internal Law of Member States', in: The British Institute of International and Comparative Law, Supplementary Publication No.11 (1965), pp.79,80-83.

6. L'application judiciaire des traités internationaux dans la Communauté européenne et dans ses Etats membres, Mélanges Teitgen (1984), pp.355-406.

makes the Convention really a meaningful and living legal instrument for those living in a particular State?

However, it is well known that the Commission and Court have not thought it possible to go as far as that.[7] The reason for this cannot be explained without taking into account the well-known distinction existing among States as to the applicability of treaty law in the municipal sphere. It is really only the fact that, from the outset, Britain and the Scandinavian States as well as Ireland did not interpret the Convention as including an obligation to make it internally applicable, which has been and had to be respected by the Convention organs. This view is expressed with great reluctance because the author is convinced that it is really a great evil that the Convention has this double standard. However, those who were the authors of the Convention must have been fully aware of the problems arising in that context and did not feel fit to include a rule which unequivocally would have made it obligatory to incorporate the Convention into domestic law.

One could of course ask whether this position should still be true forty years after the Convention has been signed. It is in fact very much this line which Judge Pescatore seems to propose. However, it is very difficult to see six important member States of the Convention who have been active in the drafting of the treaty and have been members from the very beginning as continuously in breach of their Convention obligations. Therefore, with great reluctance the view that the Convention cannot be interpreted as formally including an obligation to be incorporated into municipal law must be supported.

However, it should be noted that the European Court of Human Rights has stressed that the intention of the drafters finds a particularly faithful reflection in those instances where the Convention has been incorporated into domestic law.[8] One wonders whether time has not come to agree that this particularly faithful reflection should be the rule in all Convention States.

7. Case of *Silver and Others*, Judgment of 25 March 1983, ECHR Series A Vol.61, p.42: '... neither Article 13 nor the Convention in general lays down for the Contracting States any given manner for ensuring within their internal law the effective implementation of any of the provisions of the Convention - for example, by incorporating the Convention into domestic law'.

8. ECHR Series A Vol.25, p.91.

II. THE GERMAN SYSTEM

There follows a brief description of the German system in general.[9] Under the Federal Constitution treaties which have received the consent of the Federal Diet and where necessary the Federal Council become applicable as part of federal legislation. They have the rank of a federal statute. That means that they will have priority over all *land* legislation as well as automatic priority over all earlier federal legislation.

Theoretically, however, a later federal statute could override the rule of the Convention in internal law. In fact, we have had court decisions so holding, for instance, as far as interpreter's costs in regulatory offence proceedings were concerned until the amendment of the legislation after the *Öztürk* judgment.[10]

But the Federal Constitutional Court, in a land-mark decision of 1987, has made it very clear that, although the power of the legislature to abrogate Convention law in theory exists, it cannot be assumed that the legislature would do that. The Court held:

> In the interpretation of the Federal Constitution the content and state of development of the European Convention on Human Rights must be taken into consideration ... The case-law of the European Court of Human Rights serves as an aid to the interpretation of the content and scope of fundamental rights as well as principles of the rule of law under the Federal Constitution. Statutes - in the present case the Code on Criminal Procedure - must also be interpreted in harmony with the international legal obligations of the Federal Republic of Germany and must be so applied even if these statutes have been enacted later than the applicable treaty under public international law; this is so because it cannot be assumed that the legislature, without clearly stating so, wanted to deviate from public international legal obligations of the Federal Republic of Germany or make possible the violation of such obligations.[11]

This statement by the Federal Constitutional Court could not be clearer. In fact, it is, arguably, unthinkable that the Federal Legislature would knowingly and willingly enact statutes violating the European Convention on Human Rights. The only issue which might arise would be if a violation came about because the

9. See J.A. Frowein, in: F.G. Jacobs and S. Roberts (eds.), *The Effect of Treaties in Domestic Law* (London, 1987), pp.63-86.

10. J. Polakiewicz and V. Jacob-Foltzer, 'The European Human Rights Convention in Domestic Law', Human Rights Law Journal, 1991, pp.65,78,81.

11. Decisions of the Federal Constitutional Court, Vol.74, pp.358,370 (translation).

parliamentary draftsmen were unaware of specific obligations created by the European Convention on Human Rights.

This shows that anyone within the jurisdiction of the Federal Republic of Germany, and from the 3 October 1990 this includes of course the new '*Länder*', can argue before administrative organs or courts that his or her rights under the Convention have been violated. It is true that cases where such an argument has finally been successful are still comparatively rare. The reason for this is much less that courts or administrative organs are unaware of the Convention. It is rather that the bill of rights of the Federal Constitution which is in many respects identical with the European Convention on Human Rights will of course be the first rule applied in that context.

III. THE FEDERAL CONSTITUTIONAL COURT AND THE EUROPEAN CONVENTION ON HUMAN RIGHTS

THE more difficult issue concerns the extent to which the Federal Constitutional Court—a court with limited jurisdiction to control the compatibility of public acts with the constitution—may control other courts or administrative organs as to their application of the Convention.

The general principle which the Federal Constitutional Court announced in the decision of 1987 is a general principle of interpretation which does not in itself give jurisdiction to the Federal Constitutional Court to review court decisions on the basis of this principle.

According to its case-law as it now stands, there are two main ways in which the Constitutional Court can exercise jurisdiction, in matters where a violation of the European Convention on Human Rights could be at issue.

First of all specific rules enshrined in the European Convention on Human Rights may be seen as part of the principle of rule of law ('Rechtsstaatsprinzip'), guaranteed by Article 20 of the Federal Constitution. The principle of the rule of law in this sense is part of German constitutional doctrine and can be the basis for a constitutional complaint to the Federal Constitutional Court. In this way, constitutional complaints based on the violation of the principle of the presumption of innocence, which has always been seen as part of German law without being expressly stated in the same way as it is in Article 6 para. 2 of the Convention, have been successful before the Court. The Court has identified the rule in Article 6 para. 2 of the Convention with the 'Rechtsstaatsprinzip' of Article 20 of the Federal Constitution.

In a recent case decided in 1990 the Constitutional Court held:

> The constitutional complaint is well-founded. The decision concerning costs violates the applicant in her fundamental right under Article 2 in conjunction with the principle of rule of law of the Federal Constitution because the District Court has not respected the presumption of innocence as enshrined in the Constitution.[12]

There is, however, another road which is open for the Federal Constitutional Court to control the compatibility of public acts with the European Convention on Human Rights. Since 1983 there have been several indications that the Court may use the principle of equality under the law where German courts have not taken into account the Convention and where this must be considered to be an arbitrary decision.[13]

IV. THE IMPORTANCE OF THE CONVENTION IN PRACTICE

As already indicated the impact the Convention has had on German legal and judicial practice must be seen in the light of the rather extended guarantees of the fundamental rights in the Federal Constitution. For a long time the view prevailed that the German bill of rights could hardly offer less protection than the Convention in any area. This has proved to be untrue, as the judgments of the European Court of Human Rights concerning Germany easily show. However, even after this development it would seem to be clear that for instance as far as freedom of expression and freedom of the press are concerned German courts will mainly argue on the basis of Article 5 of the Federal Constitution which is the parallel norm to Article 10 of the Convention. If in the case of *Barthold* the German courts, including the Federal Constitutional Court, came to a result which was in violation of Article 10 of the Convention this was in fact not because they did not take into account the wording of Article 10.[14] They would have argued in the same way concerning Article 10 as they did concerning Article 5 of the German Constitution. In an area such as freedom of expression or freedom of

12. Decision of 29 May 1990, Vol.82, p.106.

13. More in detail J.A. Frowein, Das Bundesverfassungsgerichtund die Europäische Menscheenrechtskonvention, in: Festschrift für W. Zeidler (1987), pp.1763-1774.

14. ECHR Series A Vol.90, Judgment of 25 March 1985.

the press it is in the nature of things that one may have different views as to the limitations of the rights.

This is rather different in some areas where the Convention rights are clearly more explicit than the fundamental rights in the Federal Constitution which is especially the case as far as Articles 5 and 6 are concerned. One may say that two guarantees enshrined in Article 6 have been at the centre of German court decisions concerning the Convention. This is the guarantee of trial 'within a reasonable time' in Article 6 para. 1 and the principle of the presumption of innocence in Article 6 para. 2. German courts have applied the rule that a trial must terminate within a reasonable time in different respects. They have clearly underlined the obligation of all judicial organs flowing from the Convention. They have also developed the rule according to which a criminal court, when deciding on the sentence, must take into account whether the procedure has overstepped the limits of Article 6 para. 1. There are many cases where courts have clearly stated that they mitigated the sentence because of this fact.[15]

However, a more recent development shows that in extreme cases German courts will have to terminate the criminal proceedings without coming to a final judgment if the guarantee has been violated in a very severe manner.[16] The Federal Court of Justice on 9 December 1987 ordered that a criminal procedure be terminated since an arbitrary and serious violation of the rule of speediness was established. A judgment by a lower court rendered in December 1981 was communicated to the Federal Court of Justice for a decision on the appeal procedure in June 1987. Several decisions by German courts including courts of appeal have applied the rule pronounced by the Federal Court of Justice in the decision.

The other rule which has given rise to quite important case-law is the rule on the presumption of innocence in Article 6 para. 2. The Federal Constitutional Court has stated in the decision mentioned earlier that without a conviction a court may not, when terminating proceedings, speak of the guilt of a person in a decision on the costs of the proceedings.[17] This rule has been applied by many German courts although unfortunately there are still decisions which violate the Convention in this respect.

15. Comp. Polakiewicz (n.10), p.81.
16. Federal Court of Justice Criminal Cases, Vol.35, p.137.
17. *Cf.* n.12.

One has to admit that the development of the case-law in the European Court of Human Rights may not facilitate matters for the German courts. The Court in *Minelli* was very firm concerning the presumption of innocence. In the German case of *Englert*, however, the Court accepted a wording which seemed to include a statement of guilt.[18]

The Federal Constitutional Court in its decision of May 1990 has declared that a statement according to which the investigations conducted so far show that a crime has been committed violates the principle of the presumption of innocence. However, the Court has held that where only a suspicion is stated to still exist this does not amount to a violation of Article 6 para. 2.[19] It is not without some importance to realise that the President of the 2nd Senate of the Federal Constitutional Court dissented from the latter holding stating that it is impossible to make a distinction between the establishment of guilt on the one hand and a suspicion expressed in the way that guilt is highly likely.

The Federal Court of Justice has also used Article 6 para. 3(c) of the Convention to ensure that if at all possible the date for a trial must be arranged in the way that the accused is represented by his chosen counsel.[20]

Under German law, unfortunately, there is no possibility for revision when the European Court of Human Rights has held a German judgment to be in violation of the Convention. It is frequently discussed whether one should not introduce such a possibility but at the moment this does not exist.

V. CONCLUSION

YOU may ask whether the German example points in one or the other direction. If it is compared with Austria or Switzerland, where the Convention has been responsible for many decisions by national courts, the overall picture is much more doubtful. It must be realised, however, that Austria and Switzerland have bills of rights which date back into the last century in the Austrian case, or consist only of a few rights as in the Swiss example.

It is therefore quite natural that Austrian and Swiss courts have had to use many of the Convention rights to bring the case-law into line with the Conven-

18. *Minelli* case, Judgment of 25 March 1983, ECHR Series A Vol.62; *Englert* case, Judgment of 25 August 1987, ECHR Series A Vol.123.

19. As n.12.

20. Federal Court of Justice, Judgment of 8 January 1988, Juristenzeitung 1988, p.472.

tion. In Austria this is all the easier since the Convention has the rank of constitutional law.

It is the author's opinion that German courts should in fact turn to the Convention more often. However, it must be admitted, that the very active development of fundamental rights by the Federal Constitutional Court makes it in many respects unnecessary to use Convention rights or the case-law of the Convention organs.

Finally one argument is apparently still prominent with English lawyers. That is the argument according to which such vague and broad rules as the Convention rights or rights in constitutions cannot be properly applied by judges without creating dangers for legal certainty. However, it would seem to me that with the complex social developments which we face in the latter part of the twentieth century the legislature is necessarily unable to foresee all the problems, even concerning fundamental rights.

It is, therefore, of great importance that courts are able to turn to what one may call the conscience of the legal order to verify whether a piece of legislation or another public act in a specific case goes beyond what the fundamental rights of the individual permit.

Chapter 2

DOES THE CONVENTION MACHINERY DISTINGUISH BETWEEN STATES WHICH HAVE AND HAVE NOT INCORPORATED IT?

H.C. Krüger

THIS PAPER examines the scope and effect of incorporation of the European Convention on Human Rights into domestic law from the point of view of the Strasbourg organs. Does the Convention machinery distinguish between those States which have incorporated the Convention and those which have not? This subject will be dealt with in the light of the text of the Convention, the substance of the law as it is stated in the decisions of the Commission and the Court of Human Rights, and the statistics. In particular an attempt is made to answer the question whether any conclusions can be drawn from the fact of incorporation or non-incorporation as regards the availability of the complaints procedure in Strasbourg, its scope of review, and the finding of violations of the Convention.

I. THE TEXT OF THE CONVENTION

THE text of the Convention refers to the domestic law in many places. Some examples will illustrate this.

Article 1 of the Convention provides that the High Contracting Parties 'shall secure to everyone within their jurisdiction the rights and freedoms' defined in the Convention. In the *Ireland v. United Kingdom* judgment of 18 January 1978[1] the Court observed the following:

1. Series A No.24, p.91, para.239.

> By substituting the words "shall secure" for the words "undertake to secure" in the text of Article 1, the drafters of the Convention intended to make it clear that the rights and freedoms set out in Section I would be directly secured to anyone within the jurisdiction of the Contracting States (document H (61) 4, pp. 664, 703, 733 and 927). The intention finds a particularly faithful reflection in those instances where the Convention has been incorporated into the domestic law ....

Article 17 of the Convention stipulates that no State has a right to 'engage in any activity or perform any act aimed at the destruction of any of the rights and freedoms set forth [in the Convention] or at their limitation to a greater extent than is provided for in the Convention'. The national law may, however, be more favourable than the Convention standard and in this case Article 60 provides that the Convention may not be used as an argument for the limitation of, or derogation from, the more favourable protection of human rights on the domestic level.

Both the decisions of the Court and the resolutions of the Committee of Ministers are binding on the State concerned and thus entail the obligation to bring the national law into line with the Convention. However, the obligation to bring the domestic law into conformity with the requirements of the Convention makes allowance for the fact that the domestic law does not always give full redress to persons whose Convention rights have been found to be violated. Article 50 of the Convention in fact envisages the situation that the internal law 'allows only partial reparation to be made for the consequences' of a decision or measure found to be in breach of the Convention. In this case the Court may afford just satisfaction to the injured party. The system of compensation obtainable through proceedings in Strasbourg starts therefore from the premise that the national law might not provide for the removal of all consequences of a violation of the Convention in a particular case.

These provisions show that there may be some discrepancies between the national law and the Convention. They are based on the assumption that the Convention may be implemented by the Contracting States in various different ways.

However, the provisions cited above do not address the question whether the implementation system required by the Convention demands incorporation of its substantive provisions into the domestic law, or whether a system in which the Convention as such does not become part of the domestic law is also permitted. This question has been primarily examined in the light of Article 13 of the Convention which provides:

> Everyone whose rights and freedoms as set forth in this Convention are violated shall have an effective remedy before a national authority notwithstanding that the violation has been committed by persons acting in an official capacity.

Some of the earlier legal writings expressed the opinion that this provision requires a remedy by which the Convention itself can be pleaded before the domestic authorities concerned. However, this view has not been adopted in the case-law of the Convention organs. It is now established that the text of the Convention does not impose any obligation on the High Contracting Parties to incorporate the Convention rights into their domestic law.

Already in the *Swedish Engine Drivers' Union* case the Court stated in its judgment of 6 February 1976:[2]

> ... neither Article 13 nor the Convention in general lays down for the Contracting States any given manner for ensuring within their internal law the effective implementation of any of the provisions of the Convention.

This principle was repeatedly confirmed by the Court, for example, in the *Silver* judgment of 25 March 1983,[3] where it is stated:

> ... the application of Article 13 in a given case will depend upon the manner in which the Contracting State concerned has chosen to discharge its obligation under Article 1 directly to secure to anyone within its jurisdiction the rights and freedoms set out in section I.

In the *James and Others* judgment of 21 February 1986[4] and in the *Lithgow and Others* judgment of 8 July 1986[5] reaffirms this approval:

> Although there is thus no obligation to incorporate the Convention into domestic law, by virtue of Article 1 of the Convention, the substance of the rights and freedoms set forth must be secured under the domestic legal order, in some form or another, to everyone within the jurisdiction of the Contracting States ... Article 13 guarantees the availability within the national legal order of an effective remedy to enforce the Convention rights and freedoms in whatever form they may happen to be secured.

2. Series A No. 20, p.18 para.50.
3. Series A No. 61, p.42 para.113.
4. Series A No. 98, p.47, para.84.
5. Series A No. 102, p.74, para.205.

In the *Boyle and Rice* judgment of 27 April 1988,[6] the court stated:

> Article 13 guarantees the availability of a remedy at a national level to enforce—and hence to allege non-compliance with—the substance of the Convention rights and freedoms in whatever form they may happen to be secured in the domestic legal order.

The substantive approach also appears from the *Klass* case, where the Court, in its judgment of 6 September 1978[7] regarded it as sufficient for the purposes of Article 13 that the German Federal Constitutional Court had 'examined the applicants' complaints with reference not to the Convention, but solely to the Basic Law', having regard to the consideration:

> that the rights invoked by the applicants before the Constitutional Courts [were] substantially the same as those whose violation was alleged before the Convention institutions.

The same principle was also stated in regard to the implementation of other provisions of the Convention. Thus in the case of the *National Union of Belgian Police* the Court held in its judgment of 27 October 1975[8] that freedom of association under Article 11 para. 1 must be interpreted as requiring 'that under national law trade unions should be enabled, in conditions not at variance with Article 11, to strive for the protection of their member's interests'. The specific right claimed in this case, the right of trade unions to be consulted by the State, was found to be outside the scope of Article 11 because not all Contracting States 'incorporate it in their national law and practice' and because Article 11 para. 1 ' leaves each State a free choice of means to be used to this end'. In the *Schmidt and Dahlström* case[9] the Court, in its judgment of 6 February 1976, arrived at the same conclusion with regard to the question whether the right to strike was included in the guarantees of Article 11.

The doctrine of margin of appreciation developed by the Convention organs for the interpretation in particular of the limitation clauses in Articles 8-11 of the Convention, may be said to be an expression of the same principle. In the

6. Series A No. 131, p.23 para.52.
7. Series A No. 28, p.30, para.66.
8. Series A No. 19, p.18, paras.38-39.
9. Series A No. 21, p.36, para.36.

Handyside case the Court, in its judgment of 7 December 1976 observed, *inter alia*, this:

> The Convention leaves to each Contracting State, in the first place, the task of securing the rights and freedoms it enshrines ...
> Article 10 para. 2 leaves to the Contracting State a margin of appreciation. This margin is given both to the domestic legislator ("prescribed by law") and to the bodies, judicial amongst others, that are called upon to interpret and apply the laws in force ....
> 49. Nevertheless, Article 10 para. 2 does not give the Contracting States an unlimited power of appreciation ... The domestic margin of appreciation thus goes hand in hand with a European supervision. Such supervision concerns both the aim of the measure challenged and its "necessity"; it covers not only the basic legislation but also the decision applying it, even one given by an independent court ...'[10]

It is implied in this approach that the State is in principle free, in the exercise of its margin of appreciation, to shape its legislation according to its discretion, provided only that it is in substance in compliance with the obligations undertaken in the Convention. This is also borne out in the *Lithgow and Others* judgment which concerned the State's margin of appreciation under Article 1 of Protocol 1 in enacting nationalisation legislation. The Court there observed, *inter alia*:[11]

> Because of their direct knowledge of their society and its needs and resources, the national authorities are in principle better placed than the international judge to appreciate what measures are appropriate in this area ... [The Court] will respect the legislature's judgment in this connection unless that judgment was manifestly without reasonable foundation.

It therefore follows from the interpretation of various provisions of the Convention, including in particular Articles 1 and 13, that incorporation of the Convention into the domestic law is not required by the Convention, but that, as the Court put it in the *Ireland v. United Kingdom* judgment,[12] incorporation is 'a particularly faithful reflection' of the idea that the Convention rights should be directly secured to everyone within the jurisdiction of the Contracting States.

10. Judgment of 7 Dec. 1976, Series A No.24, pp.22-23, paras.48-49.
11. *Loc. cit.* p.51 para.122.
12. *Loc. cit.* p.91, para.239.

II. THE SUBSTANCE OF THE DECISIONS OF THE CONVENTION ORGANS

ONLY a minority of the Contracting States have chosen not to avail themselves of 'the particularly faithful' method of implementing the Convention by incorporating it into the domestic law. Among these States are the United Kingdom, Ireland, Sweden, Norway and Iceland. All the remaining Contracting States have incorporated the Convention although in very different manners. A purview of the Strasbourg jurisprudence shows that not only is the dichotomy between incorporation and non-incorporation relevant, but also the specific manner of incorporation. The differences in this respect concern in particular the ranking of the Convention in the domestic hierarchy of norms, the power to override national legislation, including legislation enacted after the ratification of the Convention, its self-executing character, and the possibility to invoke it before specific authorities.

The fact that the implementation system is left to the discretion of the States has important consequences in particular for the application of Article 26, the rule requiring the exhaustion of domestic remedies before a case can be examined in Strasbourg. The application of this rule is primarily the Commission's task, but since the judgment in the *Vagrancy* case[13] the Court has claimed jurisdiction to rule on preliminary exceptions raised by the respondent State on the basis of Article 26. There is therefore, apart from the very voluminous case-law of the Commission, also some important case-law of the Court on the application of Article 26 and on the consequences of direct applicability of the Convention on the interpretation of Article 26.

The basic approach adopted by the Convention organs for the interpretation of Article 26 is a substantive rather than a formal one. It is the substance of any complaint raised before the Convention organs that must previously have been put before the competent domestic authorities in order to allow them to redress the situation complained of on the national level.[14]

In this context the Commission, as early as 1961 clarified in the case of *Austria v. Italy*[15] that even in a State where the Convention has been incorporated into the domestic law and can as such be invoked before the national

13. *Loc. cit.* pp.29-30, paras.47-52.
14. *Cf.* No. 712/60, *Retimag v. FRG*, Coll. 8 p.29 (3) - YB 4, p.384.
15. No. 788/61, Dec. 11.1.61, YB 4, p.117 (170 ff).

courts, it is in principle sufficient that the substance of the matter has been put before the courts on the basis of national legislation corresponding to the Convention. Concerning a complaint under Article 6 para. 3(d) the Commission observed that:

> ... if they had expressly referred to [this provision of the Convention] the young men of Fundres/Pfunders would therefore not have raised any supplementary argument but would simply have put forward one more argument which in practice coincides, by its intention, with those they derived from the [Italian] Code of Criminal Procedure; ... to all appearances, there is no reason for assuming that their appeal would, in this manner, have met with a different and more favourable reception;

On the basis of this consideration, the Commission concluded that the failure to invoke the Convention before the Italian Court of Cassation, although it would in principle have been possible, did not justify rejection of the complaint in question for non-exhaustion of domestic remedies.

The Commission subsequently applied the same principle in many cases concerning individual petitions. A few examples follow.

Thus the Commission held in the *Guzzardi* case (concerning a complaint of deprivation of liberty by reason of the applicant's assignment to compulsory residence on an island) that '... according to its established doctrine it was sufficient that the applicant should have stated "in substance" before the national authorities the complaint he is submitting to the Commission .... [E]ven where the Convention is directly applicable in the domestic law of a state (as is the case in Italy), the person concerned may also rely before the domestic courts on "other arguments to the same effect".'[16] The principle was also confirmed in Belgian cases for example in *D. v. Belgium* and *Guchez v. Belgium*.[17]

In cases concerning the Federal Republic of Germany the Commission regularly requires the applicant to seize the Federal Constitutional Court with the complaint made before the Convention organs, although the Convention cannot be pleaded before this court as it does not form part of constitutional law. The Commission is satisfied if analogous provisions of the Basic Law have been invoked before the Federal Constitutional Court, and it examines whether in fact such analogous provisions are contained in the Basic Law.[18]

16. No. 7367/76, Dec. 10.3.77, D.R. 8, p.185 (210).
17. No. 10448/83, Dec. 12.7.84, D.R. 48, p.164 (175), No. 10027/82, D.R. 40, p. 100 (117).
18. Cf. No. 1086/61, Dec. 1.3.62, Coll. 9, p.11 (15); No. 14475/62, Dec. 24.7.63, Coll. 11,

In the *Glasenapp* case[19] the Commission stated, *inter alia*:

> Although the appeal referred principally to Article 33(2) of the Basic Law, to which there is no equivalent under the Convention, it did in fact cover the scope of the applicant's present complaint before the Commission in substance and raised the question of freedom of expression. Furthermore, the Commission must take account of the pleadings which may be necessitated in domestic proceedings where a specific guarantee, not provided by the Convention, requires an applicant to plead on the basis of that specific right.

The author is not aware of any German case where the Commission has raised the question whether the applicants should have directly invoked the Convention before the ordinary courts, where this was possible, and whether the failure to do so constituted non-exhaustion.

In Italian cases concerning Article 5 para. 5 of the Convention, the Commission reversed its earlier case-law assuming that compensation could be claimed directly under this provision[20] when it discovered that this possibility seemed excluded under the case-law of the Court of Cassation [which, in the Commission's opinion, was not invalidated by a recent and isolated decision of a lower court]. In these circumstances the Commission considered that this application could not be rejected for non-exhaustion of domestic remedies, the existence of such remedies having to be examined on the merits.[21]

However, if there is a doubt as to whether or not the domestic courts would apply the Convention, the remedy must be used. *Application No. 1161/62 v. Belgium*[22] concerned a doubt on the question, not yet decided by the Belgian courts at that time, whether the Convention, being part of domestic law, took precedence over subsequent domestic legislation. The Commission rejected that case for non-exhaustion since the applicant had failed to obtain a domestic court

p. 47 (48); No. 2201/64, Dec. 16.7.65, Coll. 16, p. 72 (74); No. 2185/64, Dec. 16.7.65, Coll. 17, p. 18 (20), No. 1459/65, Dec. 10.7.67, Coll. 24, p. 47 (48), and more recently, No. 7629/76, *Krzycki v. the Federal Republic of Germany*, Dec. 14.7.77, D.R. 9, p. 175 (179).

19. No. 9228/80, Dec. 16.12.82, D.R. 30, p.132 (142).

20. No.6694/75, *Artico v. Italy*, D.R. 15 p.169.

21. No.99202/82, *Naldi v. Italy*, Dec. 13.3.84, D.R. 37, p.75; cf. also *Ciulla* judgment 22 Feb. 1989, Series A No. 148, p.18 para.44 which confirmed the Commission's views in this respect.

22. Dec. 17.1.63, Coll. 10, p.16.

decision by which the point of doubt could have been resolved on the basis of an appeal invoking the Convention directly.

Invoking the Convention directly is also necessary when this possibility, exists in domestic law and provides the only means of putting the substance of a Convention issue before the national authorities. This principle was apparently the basis of some earlier decisions of the Commission rejecting applications on the ground that the Convention itself had not been invoked.[23] It was also the basis in the Court's *Van Oosterwijk* judgment of 8 November 1980[24] concerning the alleged violation of the right to private life as a result of the failure by Belgium to take account of the change of status of the applicant who was a transsexual. The Court:

> Undoubtedly, in domestic proceedings the Convention as a general rule furnishes a supplementary ground of argument, to be prayed in aid if judged suitable for achieving an objective which is in principle rendered possible by other legal arguments ... In certain circumstances it may nonetheless happen that express reliance on the Convention before the national authorities constitutes the sole appropriate manner of raising before those authorities first, as is required by Article 26, an issue intended, if need be, to be brought subsequently before the European review bodies ....

For this reason the Court allowed the preliminary objection of the Belgian Government based on non-exhaustion of the domestic remedies, and did not deal with the merits of the case. The Commission had previously held the opposite, finding that the applicant had brought his complaints in substance before the Belgian courts and was not required to appeal to the Cour de Cassation as the remedy was an ineffective one: the court had no jurisdiction over questions of fact and was not faced with a complaint that Belgian law had been misapplied.

Recently, the same principle was again applied in the *Cardot* case judgment of 19 March 1991,[25] concerning the complaint of the applicant that he had been convicted solely on the basis of evidence obtained in other criminal proceedings against him and had not been allowed to call his witnesses. The Court allowed a preliminary objection of the French Government that in the domestic proceedings before the Court of Cassation the applicant had not relied on Article 6 para.

23. *Cf.* for example *No. 1488/62 v. Belgium*, Dec. 18.12.63, Coll. 13, p.93 and *No. 3001/66 v. Austria*, Dec. 30.5.68, Coll. 26, p.55.

24. Series A No. 40, p.17, para.33.

25. Series A No. 200, para.35.

3(d) of the Convention or at least on the general principle of Article 6 para. 1. Again the Commission had previously held otherwise finding that the applicant had properly brought the substance of the complaints which he was now making before the Strasbourg organs before the Court of Cassation.

Invoking the Convention before the domestic authorities may be difficult due to the particular organisation of the appeals procedures before the domestic instances. Irrespective of whether or not the Convention has been incorporated into the domestic law this must be taken into account in assessing the effectiveness of domestic remedies. Thus the Commission held in an earlier case against Italy that the possibility of raising the question of the conformity of legislation with the Convention was sufficiently effective to require an applicant to make use of this possibility although the individual has no direct access to the Constitutional Court whose ruling can only be sought by the ordinary court seised of the case.[26]

This reasoning would not be followed by the Commission today.[27] In Austrian cases the Commission has consistently held that an applicant is not required to suggest to the courts a reference to the Constitutional Court with a view to a review of the constitutionality of legislation.[28] The same approach was recently adopted concerning an incidental constitutional review in Turkey.[29]

These examples show that even in States which have incorporated the Convention, it will not always be possible directly to rely on it. It is sufficient that the matter has been raised in substance. Invoking the Convention directly is only necessary in those cases where this is the only possibility of bringing the substance of the matter before the domestic authorities, or where there are doubts whether the domestic authorities would in fact apply the Convention.

The latter possibility by definition does not exist in States which have not incorporated the Convention, and in these States it will therefore always be sufficient for an applicant simply to raise the substance of his complaint before the domestic authorities.

As already mentioned, it is the intrinsic aim of the domestic remedies rule to enable the State to redress any possible violation of the Convention at the national level. Having regard to the substantive approach applicable in this respect, this

26. *Cf.* No. 6452/74, *Sacchi v. Italy*, Dec. 12.3.76, D.R. 5, p.43 (51).
27. *Cf.* EC H.R., *Brozicek* judgment of 19 Dec. 1989, Series A No.167, para.34, p.17.
28. *Cf.* i.a. *Mellacher* case.
29. Nos.14116-14117/88, *Sargin and Vagci v. Turkey*, Dec. 11.5.89, D.R. 61, p.250.

aim can be achieved both in States which have and which have not incorporated the Convention. However, the former will as a rule be better equipped to avoid findings of violations of the Convention, in particular if their law provides for the Convention to take precedence over other legal norms or for the interpretation of those norms in the light of the Convention, including its interpretation by the Strasbourg Convention organs.

Of course, the possibility of applying the Convention on the national level is no guarantee that the Convention is in fact correctly applied by the national authorities. The mere fact that these authorities have based their decisions on the Convention does not deter the individual concerned from making use of his right of petition under Article 25 of the Convention, as long as he can still claim to be a victim of a violation. It is for the Convention organs to determine in each case whether the latter condition is fulfilled.

Thus in the *Eckle* case the Court rejected the German Government's preliminary objection that the applicant could not claim to be a victim of a violation of his right to the determination of criminal charges 'within a reasonable time' because the national courts had had regard to the excessive length of the proceedings when discontinuing the prosecutions. Relying on the Commission's decision in the *Schloffer* case,[30] the Court took note of the fact that the Convention formed part of the law of the Federal Republic and that therefore there was nothing to prevent the courts from holding, if appropriate, that the Convention, and in particular Article 6 para 1, had been breached. The Federal Court's case-law provided a means of doing so, since it had held that when determining sentence, the judge must take proper account of any overstepping of the 'reasonable time' requirement of Article 6 para. 1 of the Convention. However, in the particular case no court had expressly acknowledged the existence of a breach of Article 6, para. 1, and therefore the applicant could still be regarded as a victim.[31] In the *Schloffer* case cited by the Court, the Commission had come to the opposite conclusion on the facts of that case, namely that the domestic court had sufficiently taken into account the length of the proceedings when fixing the sentence and that therefore the applicant could no longer claim to be a victim of his rights under Article 6.

In the *Preikhzas* case a similar conclusion was reached by the Commission at the merits stage of the proceedings, endorsed by the Committee of Ministers of

30. No.8180/80, Dec. 16.10.80, unpublished.
31. Judgment of 15 July 1982, Series A No. 51, pp.31-32, paras.67-70.

the Council of Europe. That case concerned the length of labour court proceedings terminated by a judicial settlement which was very favourable to the applicant. The settlement was reached after the case had been declared admissible by the Commission, the parties and the German court had been informed accordingly, and it appeared that the length of the proceedings was expressly taken into account.[32]

Both in the course of the Strasbourg proceedings and after their final conclusion, the States which have incorporated the Convention may be better equipped to react quickly to the decisions of the Court or the Committee of Ministers. Thus as a consequence of the judgment in the *Bönisch* judgment of 6 May 1985[33] the Austrian Constitutional Court reviewed the constitutionality of the applicable legal provision, Section 48 of the Food Act 1975, only a few months after the Court's decision, finding it to be in breach of Article 6 of the Convention. The provision was therefore quashed and has since been replaced by new legislation.

The Constitutional Court's judgment even had consequences for another, identical provision in the Wine Act issue in the *Brandstetter* case subsequently before the Court,[34] which was equally revoked and replaced by legislation which takes into account the European Court's judgment.

The French Conseil d'Etat reacted similarly when it applied in two recent decisions[35] Article 8 of the Convention in cases concerning the removal of illegally resident aliens from France. In one case, that of a second generation immigrant with no family ties in his country of origin, the expulsion order was quashed as being in violation of Article 8 of the Convention. In the other case, that of a pregnant woman who claimed that her state of health prevented her from being removed from the country, the removal order was sustained.

Concerning consequences of the Court's judgments, reference should also be made to the *Marckx* judgment of 13 June 1979.[36] It was stated in that judgment that the obligation under Article 53 ('to abide by the decision of the Court') 'leaves to the State the choice of the means to be utilised in its domestic legal system', the Court's judgment being 'essentially declaratory' and thus not

32. No.6504/74, Report of 13.12.78 D.R. 16, p.5.
33. Series A No.92.
34. Judgment of 28 August 1991 Series A No. 211.
35. Dated 19 April 1991.
36. Series A No.31, p.25 para.58.

involving a power to 'annul or repeal' domestic provisions found to be in breach of the Convention. It was further clarified[37] that the Court's judgments have no retroactive effect because 'the principle of legal certainty which is necessarily inherent in the law of the Convention ..., dispenses the Belgian State from re-opening legal acts or situations that ante-date the delivery of the present judgment'.

The Belgian courts, apparently relying on those statements of the Court, continued to apply the contested discriminatory legislation, finding that pending the adoption of new legislation, Articles 8 and 14 of the Convention were not self-executing.[38] The relevant provisions of the Civil Code were only repealed in 1987, without retroactive effect. The consequences were challenged in a new application[39] where the Commission in its Report of 5 April 1990 again established a violation of the above provisions. This case was sent to the Court whose judgment, dated 29 November 1991,[40] contains interesting considerations concerning the obligations of Contracting States to abide by the decisions of the Court, in particular when they have incorporated the Convention into their domestic law.

III. STATISTICAL REPERCUSSIONS

THE above brief summary of the case-law shows that also States which have incorporated the Convention can have difficulties in bringing their internal law and practice into line with the requirements of the Convention and the decisions of the Strasbourg organs. However, it is certainly true that those States may be able to fulfil their obligations under the Convention more directly and in this way to prevent cases form coming to Strasbourg. Moreover, the States concerned can sometimes react more quickly and effectively to the introduction of such cases and to the decisions of the Convention organs.

The question arises whether incorporation of the Convention into the domestic law has any impact on the number and nature of applications submitted to the Strasbourg Convention organs. In general, it can be said that there seems to be no significant influence on the number of applications. The figures for States

37. *Ibid.* p.26.
38. Decision of the Court of Cassation of 10 May 1985, R.C.B.J. 41 (1987) 5.
39. No.12849/87, *Vermeire v. Belgium*.
40. Series A No. 214.

with a comparable size of population are more or less in the same range—if one compares, for instance, France and the United Kingdom or Austria and Sweden. There was a long period when United Kingdom applications seemed to be the most frequent ones, and those which had the best prospects of success. However, recently the number of French cases has overtaken those from the United Kingdom and there have also been several findings of violations of the Convention by France while the number of admitted applications from the United Kingdom has somewhat dropped. Likewise, Austria provided for some time quite a high number of cases, but in recent years Swedish cases, which were rare in the early years, have drawn close to the Austrian numbers. The tendencies which might influence the number of applications thus seem to balance each other. Individual applicants are often of course unaware of whether or not in their state the Convention is part of the domestic law.

It must nevertheless be assumed that in States where the Convention has been incorporated into the domestic law a number of cases can be resolved on the national level with direct reference to the Convention, and that this will reduce the number of applications to Strasbourg. On the other hand, the lawyers practising in such jurisdictions are more familiar with the Convention and the case-law based on it, which provides them with a tool in their daily work, and this will probably lead to an increase of applications, all the more so as it is easy to pursue a case in Strasbourg which has already been prepared at home on the basis of the same legal argument. In some cases the application to the Commission is in fact no more than a copy of a previously unsuccessful complaint to the Supreme Court or the Constitutional Court.

Lawyers from non-incorporation countries (or countries like Germany where the Convention cannot be pleaded before the Constitutional Court) are as a rule compelled to develop new legal arguments for Strasbourg, and this might have a certain limiting effect. On the other hand, the Convention proceedings in Strasbourg may also more frequently be used as a substitute for remedies which do not exist on the domestic level. This has been very clearly stated by the applicants in the British Nationalisation cases in their pleadings before the Court.

IV. CONCLUSION

In conclusion, it may be said that incorporation is certainly desirable as it represents a 'particularly faithful reflection' of the aim to secure the Convention rights to everyone within the jurisdiction of the Convention States. It may also provide the best tool for these States to put things right in their own sphere, and to prevent too much interference by the 'foreign judges' in Strasbourg. However, as experience shows, incorporation does not provide an absolute protection against European supervision. States which have incorporated the Convention into their domestic law are also often confronted with difficult problems concerning the correct application of the Convention, both at home and in Strasbourg, and statistics do not reveal that in this respect they are much better off than States which have not incorporated the Convention. Very much seems to depend on the particular system of incorporation, for example, the availability of domestic procedures which cover all possible aspects of the application of the Convention, and which allows the judicial authorities to take into account as fully as possible not only the text of the Convention itself, but also the case-law of the Strasbourg Convention organs which in any event will have the last word on the issues brought before them.

SECTION II:

SOME NATIONAL APPROACHES TO INCORPORATION OF THE CONVENTION

Chapter 3

NORWEGIAN PROBLEMS OF COMPLIANCE WITH THE CONVENTION AND NORWEGIAN PERSPECTIVES ON INCORPORATION OF THE CONVENTION

Judge Rolv Ryssdal

I. INTRODUCTION

THE European Convention on Human Rights does not institute a system intended to replace national human rights protection. On the contrary the Convention system is of a subsidiary nature. This is reflected in the rule that no State has to answer before the Convention bodies before it has had an opportunity to redress the alleged wrong within the context of its own legal order. A number of States have incorporated the Convention into their domestic law, but the Contracting States are not required to do this in order to enable their authorities to secure the rights and freedoms guaranteed. However, even in Contracting States where the Convention is not incorporated into national law, it is, of course, a legally binding instrument, and the Convention as interpreted by the Convention institutions will accordingly have an impact upon the domestic legal system.

Norway has belonged to the so-called 'dualist' States. According to the traditional doctrine international law is binding **on** Norway, not **in** Norway. If a binding treaty is to have the force of 'the law of the land' a specific legal basis is required. In principle, two techniques are employed: 'transformation' implies the enactment of Norwegian provisions of a corresponding content, whereas 'incorporation' means that a domestic provision explicitly refers to international law by stating that national law is to be applied in conformity with international law. If these techniques have not been used, the courts may nevertheless take international law into account because of the so-called principle of presumption: it is presumed that there is no contradiction between national and international law, and the courts will accordingly endeavour to interpret the domestic law in conformity with the solution required by international law. (Instead of the rather passive expression 'principle of presumption' one should perhaps use the more active expression 'principle of the effectiveness of legally binding instruments').

Literature on the legal status of human rights conventions in Norwegian law is extensive. According to the traditional view, domestic law will prevail in case of a conflict. On the other hand, several authors have expressed themselves in favour of the opposite solution. As regards my own view in a public lecture in 1981 I said that if a conflict should arise between national legislation and provisions in a binding convention on human rights, I would think that it could be argued that precedence should be given to the Convention provisions.

As this paper tries to demonstrate, it does not give the full picture briefly to state that Norway is a 'dualist' country.

II. NORWEGIAN PROBLEMS OF COMPLIANCE WITH THE CONVENTION

AT the time of ratification the Norwegian government assumed that the domestic law was in full conformity with the Convention provisions (with one exception where Norway made a reservation). This technique is often referred to as 'the ascertainment of legislative harmony' or 'passive transformation'.

Up to now there have been no serious problems of compliance. The Norwegian authorities were perhaps to a considerable extent right in their assumption, but if as yet no real problems of compliance have occurred this is also because the so-called principle of presumption has given the Norwegian administrative authorities and courts ample opportunity to take the Convention provisions and the case-law of the Convention institutions into account.

The Supreme Court of Norway has on a number of occasions examined whether domestic law has been in conformity with Norway's obligations under the Convention.

Even in countries where the administration of justice is quite similar—as in Denmark and Norway—some traditions may nevertheless be different. The Supreme Court of Denmark for a considerable time 'overlooked' questions of compliance even if the Convention was invoked in proceedings before the Court. This may have some connection with the fact that the Supreme Court of Denmark traditionally has tended to express the reasons for its findings in a rather laconic way. The Supreme Court of Norway, on the contrary, traditionally gives detailed reasons. Whenever a breach of the Convention has been alleged, the Court accordingly has dealt with such allegations in its judgments. Some of these cases have subsequently been brought before the European Commission of Human Rights.

The first case in 1961 concerned a person who after obtaining a degree as dentist was bound to practise in Northern Norway for a limited period. He alleged that the relevant statute violated the Constitution, and he further alleged that under domestic law he was required to perform 'forced or compulsory labour' in breach of Article 4 para.2 of the Convention. The Supreme Court considered it evident that the statute did not violate the Constitution, and in the Court's opinion the provision in Article 4 para. 2 against 'forced or compulsory labour' could not reasonably be interpreted so as to comprise the work or duty at issue. The Court accordingly found no conflict between domestic law and the Convention.[1] Afterwards, on 17 December 1963, the European Commission declared a petition under Article 4 from the dentist inadmissible as being manifestly ill-founded.

Another case[2] concerned a mentally deranged person who claimed compensation because he was not allowed to be present at a public hearing. He alleged a breach of Article 6, but the Court concluded that there was no conflict between the domestic law as applied and the right to a fair hearing under Article 6.

A case in 1983[3] concerned a clergyman who was dismissed because he—as a protest against the domestic law on abortion—did not fulfil his official duties. He alleged, *inter alia*, that the domestic law was in breach of the right to life under Article 2 of the Convention. It was perhaps not necessary to deal with this complaint, but the Supreme Court made a thorough examination of his allegation. In the opinion of the Court Article 2 does not impose far-reaching restrictions on the national legislator's competence to lay down conditions for abortions, and the Court concluded that there was no conflict between the domestic law and the Convention. Later, on 8 March 1985, the European Commission declared a petition from the clergyman inadmissible as he could not claim to be a victim of the alleged breach of Article 2.[4]

1. Norsk Retstidende, that is Norwegian Law Reports, N Rt 1961 p.1350.
2. N Rt 1974 p.935.
3. N Rt 1983 p.1004.
4. *Knudsen v. Norway* No. 11045/84 DR42 p.247.

In a case in 1985[5] where the Supreme Court dismissed an appeal from a mentally deranged person sentenced to security measures, the appellant also alleged that he had been exposed to inhuman or degrading treatment in breach of Article 3 of the Convention. The Court found no basis for the view that the decision to authorise the use of security measures had violated Article 3. Later, on 7 March 1988, the European Commission declared a petition under Article 3 from the person concerned inadmissible as being manifestly illfounded, but a complaint under Article 5 para.4 was declared admissible and the case was referred to the European Court.[6]

In several other cases the Supreme Court has also examined the conformity of domestic law and practice with Norway's obligations under the Convention and concluded that there was no conflict between domestic law as applied and the relevant provisions of the Convention.[7]

In order to justify its reasoning the Supreme Court has in a number of cases not only cited the Convention as an authoritative reference text for the interpretation of fundamental rights, but also referred to or even directly relied on the case-law of the Convention institutions.

The so-called principle of presumption was thus given a particular clear expression in a judgment of 23 October 1984.[8] The point at issue was whether a person sentenced to security measures for a certain maximum period and committed to preventive detention in a mental hospital was entitled—at reasonable intervals—to a judicial review of the lawfulness of his detention. The Court first observed that neither the wording nor the drafting history of the relevant provisions gave any direct indication as to how this question should be resolved, and then went on:

> The decision to be taken must accordingly take into account all relevant circumstances, in particular the consideration that domestic law must be interpreted, as far as possible, in accordance with those treaties under international law which Norway has ratified, in this instance the [Convention].

5. N Rt 1985 p.22.
6. Case of *E. v. Norway Judgment of 29 August 1990 Series A No.181*, see below p.36.
7. N Rt 1985 p.1444 Article 5 para.1c, N Rt 1987, p.1004 Article 8 in conjunction with Article 14, N Rt 1988, p.314 Article 6 para. 3 and N Rt 1990, p.380 Article 4 of Protocol No. 7.
8. N Rt 1984 p.1175.

After a comprehensive survey of the relevant case-law of the European Court the Supreme Court concluded that its interpretation of Norwegian law on the point at issue was in conformity with the requirements of Article 5 para.4 of the Convention, as interpreted by the European Court.

Even if the formulation cited does not solve all problems which may arise, it gives a clear indication of the importance attached to the Convention and the case-law of the Convention institutions.

A civil case in 1987[9] concerned a teacher who alleged that he had been exposed to unlawful telephone tapping. He demanded a decision on the lawfulness of this alleged activity and also claimed compensation for non-pecuniary damage. The court held that any telephone tapping in the interest of national security ought to have been carried out in accordance with specific rules prescribed by law. Moreover, a control system existed under which an independent board had to examine any complaint and also had the task to secure the citizens' right to respect for private life. However, the civil courts considered it impossible to determine whether the teacher had in fact been exposed to telephone tapping because certain confidential material could not be disclosed in court. The Supreme Court referred to the European Court's judgment of 6 September 1978 in the case of *Klass and Others*, in its reasons for the non-disclosure of the confidential material in the interest of national security. Afterwards, on 8 June 1990, the European Commission declared a complaint under Articles 8 and 13 of the Convention based on these proceedings inadmissible as being manifestly ill-founded.[10]

In a case where the Supreme Court acquitted an editor of a charge of defaming a politician[11] the Court made special reference to the European Court's judgment of 8 July 1986 in the *Lingens* case,[12] and in deciding that a judge should withdraw from sitting in a criminal case[13] the Court relied on the European Court's judgment of 24 May 1989 in the *Hauschildt* case.[14]

In the field of criminal procedure the Supreme Court has repeatedly taken into account the comprehensive Strasbourg case-law concerning the right to a fair

9. N Rt 1987, p.612.
10. *P.L. v. Norway* No. 13564/88 (not yet published).
11. N Rt 1990, p.257.
12. Series A No. 103.
13. N Rt 1990, p.379.
14. Series A. No. 154.

hearing in criminal cases, and particularly the right for an accused to have examined witnesses against him protected by Article 6 para. 3d of the Convention.[15]

The judgment of 23 October 1984[16] is another example where the Supreme Court took into account the European Court's established case-law as to the requirements of Article 5 para.4 of the Convention. The case concerned a person who was committed to preventive detention in a mental hospital after being sentenced to security measures. Mentally deranged persons sentenced to security measures may, however, also be committed to preventive detention in a security ward under the prison administration. In a judgment of 11 December 1989[17] one member of the Supreme Court, Mr. Justice Smith—who as from 1 May 1991 is the Chief Justice—referred to the judgment of 1984 and added:

> I maintain that this right to judicial review which is enshrined in Article 5 para. 4 and which the Supreme Court has established for one category of persons subject to security measures, must be applied by the courts also in relation to other persons subject to such measures who are deprived of their liberty in other institutions.

The other judges did not consider it necessary to express any opinion in this respect. The question was, however, of crucial importance in the case of *E. v. Norway* decided by the European Court on 29 August 1990.[18] On the basis of a full examination of the Norwegian legal system the Court was satisfied that the available judicial review was wide enough to bear on those conditions which, under the Convention, were essential for the lawful detention of the applicant pursuant to the relevant provision in domestic law. The Court accordingly held that there had been no violation of Article 5 para. 4 as regards the scope of the Norwegian courts' power to review the lawfulness of the applicant's detention. (On the other hand the Court held that there had been a violation of Article 5 para. 4 on account of the failure to take a decision 'speedily' in court proceedings). Thus, a question of interpretation of Norwegian domestic law, which had not been decided by the Norwegian Supreme Court, had to be decided by the

15. N Rt 1990, p.312, p.319 and p.1222.
16. N Rt 1984, p.1175.
17. N Rt 1989, p.1327.
18. Fn. 6 *supra*.

European Court. There can be no doubt that Norwegian courts in future cases will follow that interpretation.

There has been no case in which the Supreme Court has been confronted with a clear conflict between the Convention and national legislation. Consequently, it has never been expressly decided whether the national norm or the Convention provision will prevail in the event of such a conflict. In earlier years the Supreme Court explicitly left this question open,[19] but such a reservation clause has not been used in later judgments.

However, it should be mentioned that a case in which there appeared to be a clear conflict was decided by the Supreme Court in 1979.[20] The case concerned a woman suffering from psychosis who was sentenced to security measures for a certain maximum period. She claimed that the period ought to be reduced, but her guardian did not consider it reasonable to lodge an appeal. According to the plain wording in the relevant provision of the Code of Criminal Procedure then in force she herself was not entitled to do so. The Supreme Court nevertheless came to the conclusion that a psychotic person able to understand the situation was competent to lodge an appeal. It would seem that this outcome—which was contrary to the clear text of domestic law—was in conformity with the Convention, but the Convention was not mentioned in the judgment.

III. NORWEGIAN PERSPECTIVES ON INCORPORATION OF THE CONVENTION

FIRST it should be mentioned that the Convention has already been incorporated into Norwegian law in some fields of considerable practical importance.

According to s.4 of the Code of Criminal Procedure of 22 May 1981 and—as from 18 December 1987—s.36a in the Code of Civil Procedure, the provisions in the two codes are to be applied within the limits which follow from recognised international law and legally binding treaties. If there were to be a conflict between a domestic procedural provision and a provision in the Convention precedence is therefore to be given to the Convention.[21] Reference should

19. N Rt 1961 p.1350 N Rt 1966 p.476 and N Rt 1974 p.935.

20. N Rt 1979, p.1079.

21. In a decision of 11 June 1991 concerning a person arrested on reasonable suspicion of having committed offences the Supreme Court expressly stated that section 183 of the code of Criminal Procedure which provides that such a person is to be brought before a court without delay and as far

further be made to s.4 of the Aliens Act of 24 June 1988, according to which the Act is to be applied in conformity with international provisions intended to strengthen the position of the individual (the alien).

Further, according to s.407.7 in the Code of Civil Procedure, a case may be reopened when the domestic final decision directly or indirectly is based on an understanding of international law which differs from that of an international court in a decision binding on Norway. In similar circumstances a criminal case may—according to section 391.2 in the Code of Criminal Procedure—be reopened in favour of the accused.

On 30 January 1989 the Norwegian Government made a decision of principle to the effect that human rights conventions binding on Norway shall be inserted into Norwegian law. At the same time it has decided that a Committee should study how such a reform ought to be implemented. The Committee was set up in December 1989 and is expected to submit its report in 1992. According to its terms of reference the Committee will have to reflect upon which conventions are to be covered by such a reform. It will also have to consider whether the insertion into Norwegian law should take the form of a general reference to such conventions or a reference to a specific convention or to certain rights. Moreover, the Committee was asked to study whether the reform should be implemented by way of constitutional or legislative amendments.[22]

I would think that the Committee in any event will recommend that the European Convention on Human Rights shall be inserted into Norwegian law. Such an insertion may take the form of an 'incorporation' *strictu sensu viz* by mere reference or by 'transformation' i.e. transcription of the substantive human rights norms into domestic provisions. The latter method may have the advantage that the rights will be formulated in the Norwegian language, possibly reformulated according to the legal technique usually employed in statutory provisions. On the other hand transformation of the Articles in the Convention can never give the full picture. Because of the principle of 'autonomy' of the meaning of the expressions used in the Convention as compared with their meaning in domestic law and also because of the 'evolutive' interpretation of the concepts stated in the Convention the method of transformation may become inaccurate or even

as possible within a day after the arrest is to be interpreted in such a way as to avoid conflict with Article 5 para. 3 of the Convention.

22. The Report of the Committee was adopted on 28 May 1993 and published in Norges Offentlige Utredninger (NOU) 1993:18. A summary is included in English (ibid. p.193).

misleading. Accordingly I would think that a reference to the Convention is to be preferred.

One may ask whether the reform should take place by way of a constitutional or a statutory amendment. The practical difference between these two solutions should not be exaggerated. Admittedly the Convention will have the force of *lex superior* if incorporation is stipulated in the Constitution. However, if the Convention is incorporated by way of a statutory provision, the legislator will certainly not by enacting new statutory provisions intend to depart from obligations under the Convention, and there is every reason to believe that the Convention will be given precedence even if there would seem to be a conflict with other statutory provisions.[23]

Given the impact of the Convention in Norwegian domestic law under the present system one may ask whether a formal incorporation will actually change the legal situation. Even if the Convention is incorporated into Norwegian law, it will not be possible to prevent doubts, shortcomings and breaches of the Convention. In this respect it is sufficient to refer to the findings in numerous Austrian and Dutch cases in spite of the fact that the Convention is regarded as constitutional law in Austria and even ranks above the Constitution in the Netherlands.

It is perhaps useful to adopt a practical rather than a theoretical approach to the question raised.

Even if the Convention has been applied in several Supreme Court decisions, its full potential has certainly not been exploited. Because of the dualistic point of departure there is reason to believe that many lawyers are still rather uncertain about the Convention's legal status in Norwegian law. Insertion of the Convention into Norwegian law would do away with the present ambiguity. An explicit provision—constitutional or statutory—will give clear guidance to those applying the law in everyday life. Such a reform will also be visible for non-lawyers and clearly demonstrate that human rights and freedoms set forth in the Convention are indeed Norwegian legal norms, and not only vague principles connected with Strasbourg proceedings. Even if it has become more and more frequent to invoke the Convention in proceedings before Norwegian courts, there is every reason to believe that incorporation will imply an acceleration of this process. If so,

23. The Report referred to in n.22 recommends incorporation of the text of the Convention into ordinary, rather than constitutional law (ibid, Chapter 10).

imperfections and conflicts will more easily be discovered. This might in turn improve the legal situation of the individual.

Another practical perspective is connected with access to information about the Convention. Since 1988, the Convention has been printed in the Collection of Norwegian Laws (Norges Lover). There is also an obvious need for easy access to case-law under the Convention, commentaries etc. In this respect steps have been taken to improve the situation. By way of illustration, a recent number of Nordic Journal on Human Rights, issued under the auspices of the Norwegian Institute of Human Rights, contained an updated register of all judgments passed by the European Court of Human Rights, systematically grouped in relation to the Articles of the Convention and its Protocols. This process will go on, but the insertion into Norwegian law of the Convention will certainly provide a fresh impetus for improvement in this field.

IV. CONCLUSIONS

THE success of the Convention system will ultimately depend on whether or not there is some form of 'co-operation' between domestic courts and the Strasbourg institutions. There is a trend in the case-law of Supreme Courts in member States to follow the interpretation of the Convention adopted by the Strasbourg Court.

Incorporation enables the national judge to consider a case under the very same provisions which may later on be at issue before the Commission and the Court. It ought significantly to reduce the need to lodge petitions in Strasbourg, and it would also provide a rich source of Convention law based on legal concepts and judicial traditions of many different jurisdictions.

On the question whether or not the Convention ought to be incorporated into United Kingdom domestic law, it would appear that an interpretative analysis of the Convention provisions by the United Kingdom judiciary would certainly be of great value not only to the Convention institutions but also to the Convention Community as a whole. However even if the Convention is not transposed into United Kingdom law, this will not, I believe, prevent the Convention provisions and the case-law of the European Court from being increasingly used as a means of interpretation whenever a clarification of an ambiguity or uncertainty in the rights and freedoms of the British citizens is required.

The reality of the Convention as a vital force in Europe is evident from the firmness with which it has taken root in the legal systems of Contracting States. This is important because the primary responsibility for the effective safeguarding of human rights and fundamental freedoms lies with the Contracting States, in particular with their judiciary.

Chapter 4

DANISH PERSPECTIVES OF INCORPORATION OF THE CONVENTION

C.A. Nørgaard

This paper first addresses the general question on the relation between international law and Danish domestic law; second, refers to Danish problems of compliance with the Convention; and, third, the main topic, examines the perspectives of incorporation of the Convention into Danish law.

I. GENERAL PROBLEMS

THE Danish constitution does not contain any specific provisions as to the effect of international law on domestic law. There is, however, a special rule which permits the transfer of powers vested in domestic authorities to supra-national organisations. International law—be it customary international law or treaties—is therefore not automatically part of Danish domestic law, but must normally be transformed into domestic law by a statute or an administrative regulation.

In some situations no specific transformation is required at all. That is the case if, after a comparison of the treaty concluded and existing Danish domestic law, it is found that domestic law is already in conformity with the treaty obligations undertaken. However, if a so-called norm-control, shows that Danish domestic law is not in conformity with a treaty obligation the treaty is normally transformed by a re-formulation of the treaty, or the part of it which requires implementation, either by a statute, or by an administrative regulation.

Under this dualist approach to the question of the impact of duly concluded international obligations on domestic law the actual implementation of these treaty obligations in domestic law, is primarily the responsibility of the legislature. It is for the legislature to provide the arrangements necessary in order that domestic law may allow for or authorise the implementation of international commitments. In practice this task is primarily carried out by the government.

The system of norm-control or re-formulation of treaties implies the risk of accidentally producing divergencies and even clear-cut conflicts between domestic law and the treaty. Such divergencies can emerge because in passing new legislation the legislature has not been aware of the potential conflict between the international obligation and domestic law, or because the scope of the international obligation has been extended as, for instance, is the case with the so-called dynamic interpretation of the European Convention on Human Rights.

However, in order to overcome such possible conflicts in specific cases the Danish domestic courts apply rules of interpretation and a presumption rule. The courts will normally attempt to interpret the national rules in such a way as to bring them in conformity with the treaty obligations. Under the presumption rule the courts may go further than would normally be possible applying the usual rules of interpretation in order to avoid a conflict between national law and the treaty obligations. This rule, of course, is based on the idea that Danish law is generally presumed to be in conformity with the international obligations which have been undertaken. It is, however, evident that the rather vague rules of interpretation and presumption cannot secure conformity of national law with international obligations in the same way as if the international treaty obligation were formally incorporated into national law.

II. DANISH PROBLEMS OF COMPLIANCE WITH THE CONVENTION

A. Legislation

Denmark signed the Convention on 4 November 1950 and ratified it on 17 April 1953. She has tried to comply with the rules of the Convention in the following way: prior to ratification the government reviewed the compatibility of Danish law with the provisions of the Convention. This review showed that in the government's view Danish law was consistent with the provisions of the Convention, although a few rules of the Statute on Social Assistance were amended. This amendment abolished the right to detain a person who failed either to support his family, or to pay alimony, or maintenance, a provision which was considered to be in conflict with Article 5 of the Convention.

Apart from this change in the legislation Danish law was considered to be in conformity with the Convention. From the discussion in Parliament it appears that Parliament and the government consider it to be beyond doubt that Danish law was compatible with the Convention.

After 1953 the practical problem has mainly been to ensure that new Danish legislation is in conformity with the rules of the Convention. This control is normally undertaken by a special department in the Ministry of Justice which checks that proposed legislation is in conformity with the Danish constitution and with international treaty obligations.

If substantial and significant legislative changes are prepared this is often achieved by the appointment by the government of a special committee of experts to investigate the whole problem and to make proposals for new legislation. It is standard procedure that draft legislation is compared with the Convention by such committees which always attempt to bring the new legislation into conformity with the rules of the Convention. The reports of such committees are normally published and numerous examples can be found of discussions and of careful consideration in order to avoid any conflict between new legislation and the Convention.

Apart from these general attempts to keep Danish law in conformity with the Convention a special problem arises if an aspect of Danish law is found not to be in compliance with the interpretation of the Convention given by the Court of Human Rights, either in judgments by which Denmark itself has been found to be in violation of the Convention or, secondly, following judgments by which other countries have been found to be in violation of the Convention. In both cases there are examples of legislative changes which have been made in order to bring the law into conformity with the interpretation given by the Court to the rules of the Convention.

With regard to cases against Denmark the situation is that up till now only ten cases have been declared admissible. In three of these cases the Commission found a violation of the Convention, but the Court did not find violation in any of these cases. In one case, however, where the Commission had found no violation, the Court found a violation; this was in the well-known—at least in Denmark—*Hauschildt* case.[1]

In his application Mr Hauschildt alleged a violation of Article 6 of the Convention on the ground that the trial judges who sentenced him to several

1. Judgment of 29 April 1986, Series A vol.154.

years' imprisonment were not impartial because they had previously taken a number of decisions concerning detention on remand in his case.

Under Danish law, detention on remand can only be ordered by a judge for a maximum of four weeks. Further detention may subsequently be ordered by a judge on the application of the prosecution, each time for a maximum of four weeks. Mr Hauschildt had been detained for a rather long period and so there had been several decisions by the judge to prolong his detention. The European Court found that Denmark had violated Article 6 of the Convention. The court said:

> In the Court's view, therefore, the mere fact that a trial judge or an appeal judge in a system like the Danish one has also made pre-trial decisions in the case, including those concerning detention on remand, cannot be held as in itself justifying fears as to his impartiality.
>
> Nevertheless, special circumstances may in a given case be such as to warrant a different conclusion. In the instant case the Court cannot but attach particular importance to the fact that in nine of the decisions continuing Mr.Hauschildt's detention on remand Judge Larsen relies specifically on Section 762, paragraph 2 of the Administration of Justice Act.
>
> The application of Section 762, paragraph 2 of the Act requires that the judge must be satisfied that there is a particularly confirmed suspicion that the accused has committed the crimes with which he is charged. This wording has been officially explained as meaning that the judge has to be convinced that there is a 'very high degree of clarity' as to the question of guilt. Thus the difference between the issue the judge has to settle when applying this section and the issue he will have to settle when giving judgments at the trial become tenuous.

The Court therefore found that in the circumstances of the case the impartiality of the said tribunals was capable of appearing to be open to doubt and that the applicant's fears in this respect could be considered objectively justified.

After the *Hauschildt* case had been declared admissible by the Commission but before the Court's judgment in the case the Danish Administration of Justice Act was amended by statute No. 886 of 10 June 1987. According to the change no one may act as a judge in the trial if at an earlier stage of the proceedings he has ordered the person concerned to be remanded in custody solely under Section 762, paragraph 2 (that is where there is a particular confirmed suspicion that the person in question has committed an offence).

After the European Court's judgment in the *Hauschildt* case, and a judgment by the Danish Supreme Court discussed further below, the Administration of

Justice Act was again amended.[2] According to the last amendment a judge cannot act in the trial if he at an earlier stage of the proceedings has ordered the person concerned to be remanded into custody if the decision to detain on remand is based on a particular confirmed suspicion *alone* or *taken together* with other reasons for detention.

Judgments by the European Court in cases against other countries have also caused changes in Danish legislation. The best example is the Court's decision in the *British Rail* case.[3]

The question of the validity of closed shop agreements in the Danish labour market has over the years been a rather sensitive one, and in some areas closed shop agreements do exist. When these matters have been discussed in Parliament, generally speaking the right wing parties have opposed closed shop agreements, whereas such agreements have been supported by the political left.

Against this background it is quite remarkable that the Social-Democratic government which was in general in favour of closed shop agreements in 1982 introduced a bill on protection against dismissal on the grounds of relations with an association. In the introduction of the bill the Minister of Labour stated that it should be underlined that with this proposal the government sought to change no more Danish law than the judgment necessitated. In the debate in Parliament the Social-Democrats stated that they were in principle opposed to the bill proposed but that Denmark of course should observe the judgment of the European Court. After a long debate the bill was enacted with only minor amendment as statute no.285 of 9 June 1982.

B. Jurisprudence of Danish Courts

Traditionally, Danish courts have been very reluctant to apply the Convention. An examination of the role of the Convention in Danish law in fact shows that it was for many years difficult to assess the value of the Convention as a source of law in court proceedings. This difficulty is attributable to sparse case material and the very brief form of the courts' decisions. It even gave rise to doubts in legal writings as to whether the Convention could be invoked at all before the courts of law.

2. By Statute no.403 of 13 June 1990.
3. *Young, James and Webster*, Judgment of 13 August 1981, Series A Vol.44.

In 1989, however, a remarkable change took place and this point has now been clarified. Three decisions of the Supreme Court[4] from the end of 1989 show that Danish courts of law and other authorities are under an obligation to base their interpretation of Danish law, to the widest possible extent, upon the European Convention of Human Rights and such practice as is incidental thereto.

The most remarkable Supreme Court decision[5] relates to the *Hauschildt* case. The case was decided in November 1989. As already mentioned, at that time the rule regarding disqualification of judges due to their involvement in earlier decisions on detention on remand was that a judge was disqualified to sit at the trial if he had ordered the person to be detained on remand *solely* on the ground that there was a particularly confirmed suspicion that the person in question had committed an offence.

In the present case a judge had decided detention on remand of three accused persons. The decisions on detention on remand were based on a combination of grounds, one of them being particularly confirmed suspicion but combined with other grounds such as risk of collusion. Before the court of appeal and the Supreme Court the question was raised whether this judge could sit as a trial judge. In its judgment the Supreme Court held that, according to the *travaux préparatoirés* of the Administration of Justice Act, the Parliament was aware of the fact that the European Commission of Human Rights in its decision of 9 October 1986 in the *Hauschildt* case had unanimously indicated that the Danish system posed serious questions as to the application of Article 6 of the Convention.

The court went on:

> Hence there is no basis for establishing that the Administration of Justice Act aims at an exhaustive regulation of the question of a judge's disqualification, because during the preparation of the case he has taken decisions concerning detention on remand.

The Court went on to say that the Act should be interpreted in accordance with the principle laid down in the judgment of the Court of Human Rights. Although the judgment is based on the particular facts and particularly refers to the number of times on which the City court judge ordered detention during the investigation,

4. Judgments of 29 Aug.1989 Ugeskrift For Retsvusen (U.F.R.) 1989 p.928, 1 Nov.1989, U.F.R. 1990 p.13 and 21 Dec.1989 U.F.R. 1990 p.181.

5. Judgment of 21 Dec.1989 U.F.R.1990 p.181.

the judgment must be interpreted as holding that it will ordinarily not be consistent with Article 6 of the Convention for a judge to participate in the trial if at an earlier stage he has ordered detention under Section 762, paragraph 2, either solely or in connection with other grounds for detention. In such circumstances the judge in question would be disqualified from sitting.

In other words the Supreme Court went rather far in its interpretation of the Danish statute and especially the word 'solely'; in fact the Court held that 'solely' did not only mean solely but meant 'solely or in connection with other grounds'.

The commentary to the judgment prepared by one of the judges who had participated in the case in the Supreme Court states that, although it was clear that a change in the prevailing practice would entail serious interference in the Danish courts' organisation of legal work and would cause organisational changes and additional expenditure for the judiciary, the Supreme Court found itself obliged to follow the decision of the European Court of Human Rights.

As already mentioned this judgment had the effect that the Administration of Justice Act was again amended so that it now reflects this Supreme Court judgment.

III. DANISH PERSPECTIVES OF INCORPORATION OF THE CONVENTION

FOR several years the question of incorporation of the Convention into Danish municipal law has been discussed in legal circles and in legal literature. In the spring of 1989 the question was brought up in Parliament and a debate took place on the adequacy of Denmark's manner of implementing the provisions of the Convention and its Protocols.

Parliament expressed doubts as to whether the Convention could actually be invoked before Danish courts of law and it was stated in several quarters that compliance with the Convention and particularly with the case law of the control organs under the Convention would be better secured if the Danish manner of execution was altered and a separate statute was adopted, thus making the Convention an integral part of Danish legislation by incorporation.

Parliament and the Danish government did not commit themselves on this issue but Parliament requested the government to set up a committee to examine the advantages and disadvantages involved in the incorporation of the European Convention on Human Rights into Danish law and to make proposals as to how incorporation technically could be achieved.

In August 1989 the Minister for Justice decided to set up an expert committee in accordance with this request.

The committee was further charged to describe the present role of the Convention and its effect on Danish legislation and, moreover, to consider whether the incorporation of the Convention would lead to a better legal protection of the individual citizen, or whether it might be considered necessary or desirable to incorporate the Convention for other reasons.

The expert committee was composed of six members, namely a representative from the Prime Minister's office, a representative from the Ministry of Foreign Affairs, a representative from the Ministry of Justice, a judge, a practising barrister and the author.

At the time when this paper was prepared the report was not yet published.[6]

I have, however, on several occasions during recent years expressed my own opinion on the question of incorporation and made clear that I am absolutely in favour of this step.

I can, therefore, briefly discuss what are generally considered to be the advantages and disadvantages connected with a possible incorporation.

The main argument in favour of incorporation is in my opinion that the incorporation of the Convention will clarify the state of the law. Even a statute solely designed to codify the practice already established by the Danish courts of law will offer a decisive advantage over the existing legal position by providing an explicit basis for the application of the Convention. The status enjoyed by the Convention in the legal system will be evident, and against a background of a more thorough knowledge of the Convention it will also be possible to generate a higher degree of awareness of the Convention principles. In my opinion, therefore, incorporation of the Convention will improve the legal protection of the individual citizen.

In the public debate and also in Parliament a number of possible disadvantages of incorporation have been mentioned.

I would like to mention three problems:

1. The question of finding a proper balance between the legislature and the judiciary.
2. The division of competence between national and international supervisory bodies.

6. The report, on the Incorporation of the European Convention on Human Rights and Fundamental Freedoms in Danish Law, was published in 1991 as Betcenkning no.1220.

3. Technical disadvantages.

A. *Balance between the legislature and the judiciary*

In the Parliamentary debate the point of view was advanced that incorporation would guarantee a step-by-step execution of the Convention according to the interpretation of its provisions by the Convention organs. By virtue of the practice adopted by these organs, the provisions of the Human Rights Convention and Protocols undergo a dynamic legislative development. As a result, the harmony between the Convention and Danish law which was perceived at the time of ratification may no longer be present.

From studies undertaken it appears that the legislature has generally been very careful to adapt national legislation to the obligations imposed by the Convention as interpreted by the Strasbourg control organs. It is extremely important that the legislature continues to adapt the Danish rules of law to the Convention on a case by case basis, regardless of possible incorporation. An incorporation statute should not be a pretext for passivity in the legislative branch with the result that the main responsibility for the practical observance of the Convention will be conferred on the judiciary. Incorporation would, however, provide a certain legal foundation for the supervisory functions of the courts which should be a kind of safety-net to ensure the correct execution of the Convention.

The European Convention on Human Rights contains a number of vague standards which leave it to the individual member State to exercise a considerable amount of discretion. The choices involved in such a political discretion should be made by the legislature and not by the courts, even where the Convention is incorporated.

An example of the interplay and balance between the legislature and the judiciary is the case decided by the Danish Supreme Court in December 1989.[7] In this case the Supreme Court considered whether it was contrary to the principle of an impartial tribunal in Article 6 of the Convention that a judge should pass sentence on a defendant charged with drug trafficking when she has prior to this passed sentences on several other persons charged with purchasing drugs from that defendant.

The Supreme Court found that, in the light of the judgment of the European Court of Human Rights in the *Hauschildt* case, it was doubtful whether the

7. See n.5.

normal Danish practice whereby the same judge for practical reasons passes sentences on all the persons charged in the same case was in accordance with Article 6.

Considering the far-reaching consequences for the organisation of the courts in Denmark which such an interpretation of Article 6 would entail, in particular of courts with only one judge, the Supreme Court, however, found that the question should be resolved by the legislature and not by the Supreme Court. The Supreme Court consequently held that the principle of impartiality had not been violated on the facts.

Even after the possible incorporation of the Convention the courts could and should continue this cautious attitude to an independent interpretation of the Convention, notably in cases where such an interpretation might have far-reaching consequences for the state of the law. Such a cautious attitude by the courts would ensure that the balance between the legislature and the judiciary would not be disturbed by incorporation.

B. The division of competence between national and international supervisory bodies

As an argument in favour of incorporation it has been stated that a larger number of cases would be likely to be finally decided by a national court of law if this court was in a position to apply the Convention directly. Both the contracting State and the citizens affected will normally benefit from the settlement of human rights issues at a national level, one of the reasons being the avoidance of prolonged investigation by the control organs under the Convention. Moreover, in the event that a complaint is referred to those organs, it must be important that all aspects of the complaint, including aspects relating to the Convention, have been considered by the national courts.

Against this point of view it has been argued that some of the decisions necessitated by the application of the Convention can be made only by the control organs under the Convention. This is, for instance, relevant in connection with Articles 8 - 11 of the Convention which lay down that national provisions, which place restrictions on the exercise of the rights, are only compatible with the Convention if necessary in a democratic society.

It has been argued that if the Convention was incorporated and Danish courts had to decide whether or not a concrete restriction was necessary in a democratic society in cases where no practice from Strasbourg had been established, uncertainty would be created. Such uncertainty could be detrimental to the individual applicant in cases where the Danish courts found no violation of the Convention and where the complainant consequently decided not to bring the matter to Strasbourg on the assumption, possibly wrong, that the matter had been finally settled by the Danish court, or at least settled in a manner which would not strengthen the complainant's position in Strasbourg.

On the other hand, it has been argued that the government or governmental organisation may run the risk that a Danish court of law finds a conflict with the Convention even if its finding is not based on the practice of the control organs under the Convention. The State will not be entitled to bring such a national court decision before the control organs under the Convention but will have to abide by the decision of the national court.

As far as the latter objection is concerned the situation would be most unlikely to occur on any major scale. Further, where a governmental organisation is incapable of convincing the domestic court of the correctness of an interpretation there will normally be no reason to assume that the State will be more successful in a case before the control organs of the Convention.

As far as the first objection is concerned, where a citizen accepts a theoretically wrong interpretation of the Convention, it will in any event be up to the individual citizen to decide whether he or she wishes to bring a matter of human rights before the Convention organs. It is not the duty of the State in question to make sure that all cases where there might be a human rights issue are brought before the organs under the Convention, irrespective of the interest of the person in question. On the contrary, it will basically be an advantage for the citizens, as part of their duty to exhaust local remedies, to be offered the possibility of hearing the national court's interpretation of the human rights aspect involved in the case.

C. *Technical disadvantages*

It has been argued that an incorporation statute will take the form of a supplementary act in relation to other legislation and therefore be alien to the system. Under normal circumstances, provisions on imprisonment will be looked for in the Administration of Justice Act and provisions on the minimum age for marriages will be looked for in the Contracting and Dissolution of Marriage Act, but both issues are governed by the Convention and the Protocols to the

Convention and an incorporation statute will apply as a supplement to the existing statutes which will not be amended.

There may be some force in this argument as being a departure from the generally accepted principle on the drafting of legislation. However, no major importance should be attached to such departure, partly because it is an inevitable consequence of the fact that the incorporation takes place at a time when the Convention has been implemented in another manner for a considerable number of years. In the future, however, the relevant legislation should be adapted to the obligations imposed by the Convention as interpreted by the control organs. An incorporation statute is designed to clarify that the national provisions are based on international law and to establish the binding nature of such provisions.

Finally, it has been argued that if the Convention were incorporated there would be a very high demand for information and education about the Convention. This is true and it may, at least for a certain period, create some extra work for lawyers in private practice or in public service. In order to meet the demand for information specific arrangements must be made. In fact this is a problem which the Danish expert committee has dealt with, making proposals as to how information could be provided in an efficient and practical way.

It is the author's view that the Convention should be incorporated into Danish law by way of a statute. Further, it is suggested that the rights safeguarded under the Convention are also an integral part of the EC law including community provisions to be administered by Danish authorities. The practical importance of this is still presumably quite modest, but in principle it is of major significance that the law-applying authorities pay attention to views on human rights as a potential corrective to an interpretation of community laws and national laws which could otherwise appear obvious. Finally, the inclusion of human rights into community law throws a new light upon the question of incorporation.

The question, in fact, is no longer whether the Human Rights Convention should be incorporated into Danish law, but to what extent this should be effected, in other words whether the incorporation process should be expanded t[illegible]clude spheres that do not relate to the implementation of community [illegible]ons.[8]

By Statute no.285 29 Apr.1992 which entered into force on 1 July 1992 the Convention was [illegible]orated into Danish law.

Chapter 5

DRAFT LEGISLATION TO INCORPORATE THE EUROPEAN CONVENTION ON HUMAN RIGHTS INTO UNITED KINGDOM DOMESTIC LAW

Robert Blackburn

THIS chapter aims to give a picture of the progress made in Britain on legislation designed to embrace the Convention into our legal system. It will explain the stage which draft legislation has reached at Westminster, and give details of the contents of the parliamentary Bills as most widely supported. It will then look at legislative or parliamentary opinion on the desirability of incorporation especially inside the House of Commons. The policy arguments adopted are largely political in tone, as opposed to the more legalistic arguments discussed so far in this book.[1]

I. PROPOSALS MADE

IT can fairly be said that the form of draft legislation is now at an advanced stage. The drafting of recent Bills presented to Parliament for debate has been the product of wide consultation and legal experience, and in my view the *Human Rights Bill*[2] which is discussed below is fit to be put on the statute book straightaway.

Although legislative proposals to incorporate the Convention have been periodically put forward since the 1960s, the real landmark came on 25 March 1976 when Lord Wade moved a debate in the second chamber of Parliament on

1. See Robert Blackburn, 'Legal and Political Arguments for a United Kingdom Bill of Rights' in Robert Blackburn and John Taylor, *Human Rights for the 1990s* (1991).
2. HC [1986-87] 19.

a Bill aimed at incorporation. This led to a Select Committee of the House of Lords being set up to investigate thoroughly the implications of incorporation and sort out some legal drafting difficulties especially concerning compatibility with the principle of parliamentary sovereignty. Its Report together with the Minutes of Evidence taken from a wide number of experts was published in 1978, and still remains one of the clearest analyses of the legal and political issues involved.[3] Significantly, both Lord Wade's Bill and the Select Committee's Report were entitled 'Bill of Rights'. This is important to understand, for as Lord Browne-Wilkinson and Judge Ryssdal have argued, incorporation of the Convention by law and a constitutional bill of rights are separate concepts which do not necessarily go hand in hand. But whilst Lord Wade sought to adopt the Convention's wording and principles into United Kingdom law, he also wished to give their status in law superiority over ordinary later legislative enactments, and set up the judiciary as constitutional guardians of citizens' rights in Britain. Politically this is how the debate on incorporation has been viewed in this country, and virtually all legislative proposals on incorporation over the past 15 years have been directed towards this end.

How many serious attempts at legislation have there been in Parliament in recent years? A Bill to effect incorporation has been introduced into the parliamentary second chamber, the House of Lords, upon four separate occasions and passed all its stages. The most prominent of these attempts in the 1980s was the *Human Rights and Fundamental Freedoms Bill* presented by Lord Broxbourne in 1986, and which Lord Scarman helped to draft.[4] The House of Lords therefore can be said to support incorporation, but on each occasion a Bill passed by them has been sent on to the House of Commons for consideration, time has not been made available there by the government for a debate. It was highly significant then, when the Conservative MP Sir Edward Gardner obtained fifth place in the 1986-87 session's ballot of Members for Friday's reserved for Private Members' Bill business, and chose to present his *Human Rights Bill* for a second Reading debate in the Commons, which was drafted in similar terms to the

3. Report of the Select Committee on a Bill of Rights (1978), HL 176. The Committee was divided on the question of whether a Bill of Rights was desirable or not (six supported the proposal, five opposed), but was unanimous that 'if there was to be a Bill of Rights, it should be a Bill based on the European Convention of Human Rights'.

4. HL [1985-86] 21.

Human Rights and Fundamental Freedoms Bill which in the previous session had already passed through the House of Lords.[5]

Virtually all of the draft legislation produced has been the product of a co-operative effort by supporters of incorporation. Each successive Bill introduced in Parliament has been slightly modified to reflect the balance of opinion among supporters, or render the draft more acceptable to earlier opponents. For example, on the difficult issue of how the Bill might control future legislative enactments, Sir Edward Gardner included in his *Human Rights Bill* the successful amendment of Lord Lloyd of Hampstead to Lord Broxbourne's *Human Rights and Fundamental Freedoms Bill* in the previous year in the Lords. Indeed he publicly credited the drafting of the Bill to Lords Scarman and Broxbourne. The senior Liberal Democrat Member of Parliament Robert Maclennan formally supported the presentation of Sir Edward Gardner's Bill, as in turn Sir Edward Gardner had similarly supported a *European Human Rights Convention Bill* of Robert Maclennan in 1984.[6] Parliamentarians who should like to incorporate the Convention have thus effectively united around the form of legislation discussed below.

II. CONTENTS OF THE DRAFT LEGISLATION

A major advantage of the draft legislation contained in the *Human Rights Bill* is its presentational simplicity. Its nine sections run to no more than three pages.[7] Its Schedule of Rights and Freedoms are Articles 2 to 14 of the Convention together with Articles 1 to 3 of its Protocol No. 1. There are many supporters of a new Bill of Rights in this country who would like to see the principles contained in such an Act of Parliament varied, elaborated and made more precise in suit British legal conditions. The Institute for Public Policy Research's recent publication *A British Bill of Rights* is a case in point.[8] Excellent document though it is, and whilst the author would prefer the principles it contains, politically it is just not feasible to think that the political parties in the House of Commons at Standing Committee stage would do anything but get terminally

5. The debate ran out of time after five hours, and the Bill proceeded no further.

6. HC [1983-84] 73.

7. The term 'section' is used here for consistency with the text of the Bill, although it is customary for British lawyers to use the term 'clause' when speaking of draft legislation.

8. (1990).

bogged down on the interpretation and drafting of individual rights. As the different Citizens' Charter policy documents which have emanated from each of the three main parties show all too clearly, they have a widely different interpretation of which rights of citizenship are most important. The only real legislative prospect in the existing political climate is for a Bill simply to adopt the internationally respected principles of the Convention as they stand—not a variant of it. Section 2 of the draft legislation then, simply provides that the Convention's rights and freedoms 'shall have the force of law in the United Kingdom'.

Sections 3 and 8 impose a duty upon all public bodies including the Crown and Ministers not to infringe any of these rights and freedoms, and renders them liable in civil proceedings to any person within the jurisdiction of the United Kingdom who may be adversely affected. The key features here then are that not just British citizens but any person within the United Kingdom may petition, and the scheme is limited to actions against public authorities, not private bodies too. However 'public authority' is construed in the interpretation clause in section 1 as a 'body of persons, whether corporate or unincorporated, carrying on a service or undertaking of a public nature', so this liberal meaning would extend for example to the recently privatised public utility companies.

Section 9 deals with the problem of derogation, in other words the emergency circumstances in which public authorities may be permitted to offend against normal human rights standards. The clause says that the constraints of such individual rights and freedoms upon governmental activity will be lifted 'if at any time Her Majesty declares by Order in Council that there exists a state of war or other public emergency threatening the life of the nation'. However such derogation would not be permitted over the European Convention's Articles 2 (except in respect of death resulting from lawful acts of war), 3, 4 (paragraph 1) and 7. Any such derogating measures therefore should be in the form or Orders in Council, which subsection (2) states may not be questioned in any legal proceedings.

The statutory machinery created by the draft legislation includes no special court to hear alleged violations of the fundamental rights and freedoms. Application to the ordinary courts is envisaged so that the Rule Committee of the Supreme Court would settle the details of jurisdiction and procedure. Neither is any Human Rights Commission created, although many would wish to see one being introduced by later legislation, with powers to investigate complaints and bring actions itself. Section 6 provides that in the interpretation of the Convention's principles, judicial notice shall be taken of the judgments of the Strasbourg Court of Human Rights, and also all published reports and decisions of the European Commission of Human Rights. Section 7 and Schedule 3 lays down that where any human rights or freedoms issue arises in any legal proceedings, the appropriate Law Officer (the Attorney-General in England and Wales, Lord Advocate in Scotland, and Attorney-General for Northern Ireland in Northern Ireland) must receive notice from the court or tribunal, and is permitted to be a party to the proceedings. A normal limitation period of six months in which to commence any such civil action alleging a human rights violation is imposed by section 5.

Finally, section 4 addresses the conundrum of how the fundamental rights and freedoms can be made to control future legislative enactments. Under Britain's unwritten constitution of course, there is no concept of fundamental law superior in status to ordinary acts of Parliament. If there is a conflict between two statutes, regardless of the former purporting to render what the latter seeks to do unlawful, the later statute always prevails. This is the traditional doctrine of parliamentary sovereignty as so called by Professor Dicey at the end of the last century.[9] However European Community law has *de facto* come to be made to prevail, as it was clearly intended to do by section 2(4) of the European Communities Act 1972, by the British judiciary taking that entrenchment clause to lay down a very strong rule of interpretation, so that Parliament in its legislation is presumed not to have intended to legislate contrary to Community law. It seems it may be a presumption that can only be displaced by the later statute expressly stating that it is passed in repudiation of Community law.[10] Section 4 of the draft legislation to incorporate the Convention seeks to achieve a similar effect. It reads,

> No provision of an Act passed after the passing of this Act shall be construed as authorising or requiring the doing of an act that infringes any of the fundamental rights and freedoms, or as conferring power to make any subordinate instrument authorising or requiring the doing of any such act, unless such a construction is unavoidable if effect is to be given to that provision and to the other provisions of the Act.

9. *The Law of the Constitution* (1885).
10. For example see Lord Denning's *dicta* in *Macarthys v. Smith* [1981] 1 All ER 111 at 120.

Thus section 4(2) side-steps British legal dogma by instead laying down a rule of statutory interpretation: essentially it invites the judiciary to interpret all later subordinate and primary legislation upon the presumption that Parliament does not intend to legislate in contradiction to the European Convention on Human Rights' principles. But if ever an Act of Parliament made it clear it was to take effect notwithstanding the fundamental rights and freedoms, then that later legislation would prevail, and thus the theory of parliamentary sovereignty remains intact.

III. PARLIAMENTARY OPINION

THE official view of the present British government is opposed to incorporation of the Convention. When Margaret (now Baroness) Thatcher, then Prime Minister, was asked in a parliamentary question whether the government would support incorporation, as a United Kingdom Bill of Rights, she responded in typically forthright fashion, 'No'. She went on to explain that the Conservative government 'are committed to, and support, the principles of human rights in the European Convention but we believe that it is for Parliament rather than the judiciary to determine how these principles are best secured'.[11]

The most frequently cited argument against incorporation is that it would politicise our judges, thereby damage their reputation for impartiality and independence in the perception of ordinary citizens, and consequently erode popular confidence in the courts and legal system as a whole. Thus the former Attorney General, Sir Patrick Mayhew, has said this is the principal factor in the Government's view of the proposal. In a parliamentary debate he said,

> The judiciary must be seen to be impartial. More especially, as far as practicable it must be kept free from political controversy. We must take great care not to propel judges into the political arena. However, that is what we would do if we asked them to take policy decisions of a nature that we ought properly to take ourselves and which under our present constitution we do take. We would increase that danger if we required or permitted them to alter or even reverse decisions taken by Parliament. For a long time I have felt that herein lies the key to the general issue that we are debating'.[12]

11. HC Deb., Vol.156, Cols.251-252.
12. HC Deb., Vol.109, Col.1267.

Other commonly expressed views at Parliament are that British judges are not used to, or equipped to deal with, broad statements of principles such as those in the European Convention; that British judges are too executive or Establishment—minded to be entrusted with balancing the rights of the individual against the State; and that incorporation would lead to an explosion in the number of cases brought in the already heavily overburdened High Court ('a myriad of cases by a lot of crackpots' as Lord Denning surmised in one House of Lords debate).[13] A far more potent concern, but one which has only been identified and articulated by one MP in the Commons to my knowledge, is that incorporation may in practice interfere with MPs' ability to take up and pursue some individual grievances on behalf of their constituents directly with Ministers: for the government would be able to argue that this is not a matter for MPs or the House of Commons, but should be pursued through the courts of law.

The views of supporters at Westminster of incorporation have been reflected in many of the contributions already expressed in this book. A more general sentiment is that the British constitution is simply out of date, especially in lacking any legal statement of basic citizens' rights and freedoms. According to the former Liberal leader, Sir David Steel, the balance of the constitution and sheer scope of governmental activity has changed over the past decades, so that new devices were now needed to protect the individual. 'Parliament on its own can no longer adequately protect our citizens. The increase in the executive arm of Government and in the number of areas of Government activity, under Governments of all parties, and the increasing complexity and speed of modern life have meant that the individual is in need of greater protection, but is afforded less'.[14]

Many MPs have expressed the view that it is shameful to have so many rulings against the United Kingdom at the Strasbourg Court, when it is most likely that the same results would have been reached by a British court obliged to apply the Convention's human rights principles. Others have stressed the practical limitations of the European machinery to the ordinary citizen in the United Kingdom, given the legal costs and length of time involved in presenting a case to the Commission and to the Court. Even after a victory in the Strasbourg Court, coming after anything from four to six years' litigation, 'no doubt that is a triumph morally' to quote Lord Scarman, 'but it is not very useful

13. HL Deb., Vol.469, Col.172.
14. HC Deb., Vol.109, Col.1232.

to the citizen after so much delay'.[15] The main parliamentary consensus of support however, is the simple proposition that there should be incorporation of the Convention's principles into British law, so as to entitle the citizen to positive, actionable rights in the courts, and so enable the ventilation of grievances and complaints through the judicial process about fundamental rights and freedoms.

IV. PROSPECTS FOR INCORPORATION

In conclusion, what is the level of political support and likelihood of incorporation? There is no doubt that there is now very strong and wide support for incorporation, across the political parties, across the legal profession,[16] and also in popular terms. Certainly the level of support is now greater than it has ever been. Politically it is an issue that cuts across party political lines. The Liberal Democrat Party as a whole is committed to incorporation. Although the Conservative party leadership is formally opposed, yet there are many of its members such as Sir Edward Gardner who are for it, and several former Conservative Cabinet Ministers have at various times publicly proclaimed their backing, including Lord Hailsham, Sir Leon Brittain, and Lord St. John of Fawsley. The new Chairman of the influential House of Commons' Home Affairs Committee, the Conservative Sir Ivan Lawrence, is a supporter. More Labour politicians are for incorporation than ever before, and its front bench policy, formerly against, is now at worst ambivalent. The former Labour Party Deputy Leader, Roy Hattersley, said shortly before the 1992 General Election, 'We should set out a statement of principles. They should be more than declaratory. Indeed, though inevitably general, they should possess the full force of law. Whether or not they are called a Bill of Rights is of no real consequence ... The principles would perform the Bill of Rights' basic task of establishing in law the framework of a free society'.[17] And since the 1992 Election the new Labour Leader, John Smith, has clearly stated his own personal support for incorporation. There would appear to be some electoral advantage in adopting incorporation as a party policy, for several recent leading public opinion polls

15. HL Deb., Vol.469, Col.162.

16. A recent development of particular significance is that Sir Thomas Bingham, appointed in September 1992 the new head of the civil division of the Court of Appeal as Master of the Rolls, has publicly declared his support for incorporation of the Convention.

17. Speech at South Bank Polytechnic, 1991.

have shown a clear majority of the electorate support the principle.[18] Forty years ago when the Council of Europe was born, and the Convention was agreed between member States, incorporation of its human rights principles into United Kingdom domestic law was unthinkable. But especially over the past fifteen years there has been growing support in the political and legal establishment, and it is now very firmly on the parliamentary agenda for further consideration. It is a legal change of great imporance that has every prospect of being finally enacted before the end of the 1990s.

18. See e.g. MORI poll conducted for the Constitutional Reform Centre in 1985, and for the Joseph Rowntree Trust in 1991.

SECTION III:

ASPECTS OF THE CONVENTION'S PLACE IN THE LAW OF THE UNITED KINGDOM

Chapter 6

THE TREATMENT AND INTERPRETATION OF THE EUROPEAN CONVENTION ON HUMAN RIGHTS BY THE ENGLISH COURTS

Nicolas Bratza QC

IN a case decided in 1982 and called *Taylor v. Co-operative Retails Services Ltd*[1] the Court of Appeal was required to consider a claim by a milk-roundsman who had been dismissed by his employers, the defendants, on the grounds of his refusal to leave one union and join another in accordance with a closed shop agreement. The Court of Appeal rejected his appeal on the grounds that by the terms of the Trade Union and Labour Relations Act 1974 and the Amendment Act of 1976 his dismissal was to be treated as fair. However, in typically trenchant terms, Lord Denning expressed his view that the appellant had been subjected to a degree of compulsion which was contrary to the freedom guaranteed by Article 11 of the Convention and that the Acts of 1974 and 1976 were themselves inconsistent with the rights guaranteed by that Article. Since however the Convention was not part of our law the appellant could not recover compensation in the domestic courts. This prompted Lord Denning to add the following somewhat bleak footnote:

> If he applies to the European Court of Human Rights, he may in the long run—and I am afraid it may be a long run—obtain compensation there. So in the end justice may be done. But not here.

On the facts of that case it is perhaps difficult to argue with Lord Denning's view. What is much more debatable is the broader question whether the failure

1. [1982] I.C.R. 600.

of the United Kingdom to incorporate the Convention means that the national courts are in general unable to provide a remedy where fundamental human rights have been violated or whether the incorporation of the Convention as part of domestic law would in practice add little to the protection already afforded to the individual by statute and by the common law. This paper provides a very brief overview of the way in which the Convention has been treated by the domestic courts, even though not forming part of our domestic law. This is done by looking at the three main areas in which regard has been had to the Convention by the courts: as an aid to statutory interpretation; as guidance in the development of the common law; and in the field of judicial review.

So far as the author can discover, the Convention was first referred to in a judgment of the courts of this country in 1974 in *R. v. Miah*,[2] a case in which the House of Lords rejected an argument that the Immigration Act 1971 had created retroactive criminal offences. In delivering the only speech, Lord Reid stated that it was important to bear in mind Article 7 of the Convention and noted that in the light of that Article it was hardly credible that any Government department would promote, or that Parliament would pass, retroactive criminal legislation.

Since that date the trickle of cases in which reference has been made to the Convention by domestic courts has turned, if not into a flood, at least into a steady stream. A recent Lexis search reveals that the Convention has been referred to in the judgments of domestic courts and tribunals well over 200 times. It is true that in the majority of cases the reference has been a passing one. But what an analysis of the authorities does show is an increasing readiness on the part of the courts to consider the Convention even in cases which do not at first sight appear to raise Convention issues. One finds less commonly in the more recent judgments statements such as are to be found in the *Bibi*[3] case in 1976 to the effect that Article 8 of the Convention is 'too wide to be of practical application' and that the Convention is 'not the sort of thing which we can easily digest'.

This greater readiness to look at the Convention itself has gone hand in hand with a willingness on the part of the courts to examine the jurisprudence of the European Court and Commission and to draw on concepts developed by the

2. [1974] 1 W.L.R. 683.

3. *Reg. v. Chief Immigration Officer, Heathrow Airport, ex p. Salamat Bibi* [1976] 1 W.L.R. 979.

Convention organs. In particular, in a number of decisions relating in the main to freedom of expression, the concept of a 'pressing social need' has been invoked and applied by the domestic courts.

Having said this, it is right to add that, in the vast majority of the 200 plus cases where the Convention has been referred to, the Convention appears to have made little or no difference to the result at which the court has arrived. More often than not, the Convention has been invoked by the court to reinforce the view which has already plainly been formed by the court as to the proper outcome of the case. This is not necessarily intended as a criticism. It is true that the Convention—and more particularly the restrictions contained in paragraph 2 of Articles 8–11—have been prayed in aid as justifying the court in taking a restrictive view of the right or freedom in issue. But this has not always been the case. Particularly in the case of freedom of expression—and the judgments in and following the substantive hearing of the *Spycatcher* litigation are a good example—the Convention and Convention jurisprudence have been invoked by the courts as providing an important justification for their refusal to continue in force any form of injunctive relief.

The following sections consider the treatment of the Convention by the domestic courts in the three main areas indicated above.

A. Statutory Interpretation

The extent to which the Convention could be invoked where the provisions of an Act of Parliament were in issue was first considered by the courts in a succession of cases arising under the Immigration Act 1971. The first of these—the *Birdi*[4] case—contained the most radical statement of principle, Lord Denning going as far as to suggest, albeit obiter, that if an Act of Parliament did not conform to the Convention he might be inclined to hold it invalid. Lord Denning very quickly recanted, holding in the case of *Bhajan Singh*[5] that his earlier statement had been 'very tentative' and had gone too far. Instead, he restated the orthodox rule which has since been consistently adhered to that 'if an Act of Parliament contained any provisions contrary to the Convention, the Act of Parliament must prevail'.

4. *Birdi v. Secretary of State for Home Affairs*, 11 February 1975, Bar Library Transcript No.67B of 1975.

5. *Reg. v. Home Secretary, ex p. Bhajan Singh* [1976] 1 Q.B. 198.

In the subsequent case of *Phansopkar*,[6] Scarman LJ expressed the view, in reliance on the decision in *Bhajan Singh*, that it was:

> the duty of our public authorities in administering the law, including the Immigration Act 1971, and of our courts in interpreting and applying the law, including the Act, to have regard [to the Convention].

He added that it was the duty of the courts, so long as they did not defy or disregard clear unequivocal provisions, to construe statutes in a manner which promoted, and did not endanger those rights.

Even that relatively modest formulation was held in the subsequent case of *Bibi* to have been too widely expressed. In that case Roskill LJ took issue both with the suggestion that public authorities should be required to have regard to the Convention in administering the law and with the suggestion that the courts should consider the Convention even in a case where the statute did not expressly or impliedly incorporate it into English law.

In subsequent authorities the courts have had regard to the Convention as an aid to statutory construction even in cases where the statute could not sensibly be said either expressly or impliedly to incorporate the Convention. However, in passing note the recent decision of the Court of Appeal in the *Colman*[7] case where there is at least a suggestion that regard should be had to the Convention as an aid to statutory construction only where the subject matter of the statutory provision in question may properly be regarded as the subject matter of an international obligation under the Convention – a test which I suggest is going to be very difficult to apply in practice.

Where the courts have been consistent is in their requirement that recourse may be had to the Convention only for the purpose of resolving ambiguities: where the statute is clear and unambiguous there is no room for introducing the Convention. The point is perhaps most succinctly made by Lord Bridge in the *Brind*[8] case where he noted that:

> it is ... well settled that, in construing any provision in domestic legislation which is ambiguous in the sense that it is capable of a meaning which either conforms to or

6. *Reg. v. Secretary of State for the Home Department ex p. Phansopkar* [1976] 1 Q.B. 606.
7. *Reg. v. General Medical Council, ex p. Colman* [1990] 1 All ER 489.
8. *Reg. v. Secretary of State for the Home Department ex p. Brind* [1991] 1 A.C. 696.

conflicts with the Convention, the courts will presume that Parliament intended to legislate in conformity with the Convention, not in conflict with it.

This principle has been invoked by the courts in several cases concerned with statutory interpretation. However, an analysis of the cases shows that this potentially fruitful area for the application of the Convention has in practice proved of little value. The usefulness of the principle has been undermined by the courts' insistence that the statutory provision should be ambiguous before recourse may be had to the Convention and, it is ventured, an over–readiness on the part of the courts to hold that the words of a statute are plain and unambiguous.

A recent example is in the case of *R. v. Secretary of State for the Home Department, ex parte K.*[9] in which the Court of Appeal was faced with the question whether the Secretary of State could issue a warrant to recall a patient who had been conditionally discharged from a mental hospital in a case where there was no evidence that the patient was at the time of recall suffering from mental disorder. The power of recall was contained in section 42(3) of the Mental Health Act 1983 which was admittedly cast in wide terms. It was argued on behalf of the appellant with some justification that the section should be construed in accordance with Article 5 of the Convention and with various decisions of the European Court of Human Rights to which the 1983 Act was, at least in part, intended to give effect. The argument was rejected by the Court of Appeal on the short ground that the section was plain and unambiguous in its terms and that it was accordingly not open to the court to look for assistance to the Convention. This was so even if, as the appellant argued, the section as so interpreted was clearly inconsistent with the United Kingdom's Convention obligations.

Even in those relatively few cases where the courts have invoked the Convention as an aid to statutory interpretation, the discussion of the Convention does not appear to have affected the disputed point of interpretation. Thus, for example in *Ahmad v. I.L.E.A.*[10] a majority of the Court of Appeal held that I.L.E.A. was not in breach of section 30 of the 1944 Education Act by requiring the appellant, a Muslim, to become a part–time teacher, if he wanted time off work each Friday for prayer. The section provided, *inter alia*, that no teacher

9. [1990] 1 W.L.R. 168.
10. [1978] Q.B. 36.

should receive any less emolument by reason of his attending religious worship. It was Scarman LJ who drew attention to Article 9 of the Convention in the course of argument and who, in a dissenting judgment, held that section 30 should be broadly construed against the background of Article 9. While the majority of the Court also made reference to Article 9, they did so only after they had already expressed the view that section 30 could not be read literally and without qualification so as to entitle the appellant to take time off for his prayers without loss of pay. Article 9 was then somewhat perfunctorily dealt with on the grounds that it could not be construed as entitling an employee to absent himself from his place of work for the purpose of religious worship.

I should mention, however, one area in which the Convention **has** perhaps proved of some value as an aid to statutory interpretation, namely as to what constitutes inhuman or degrading treatment or punishment or, as it is expressed in the Bill of Rights of 1688, cruel and unusual punishment. In this context the Privy Council has on several occasions had recourse to the Convention in determining issues arising under the Constitutions of Commonwealth countries. But it has also been used by the domestic courts. In three cases involving prison treatment or condition—*Williams*,[11] *Herbage*[12] and *Weldon*[13]—Article 3 of the Convention was invoked by the Court in conjunction with the Bill of Rights in relation to complaints by the applicant that he had been subjected to unacceptable conditions of detention. It is right to say that in each of these cases the court's treatment of the Convention was cautious and that the courts were at pains to stress that the Convention standards were not part of our domestic law. Nevertheless the cases reveal at least a readiness on the part of the courts to have regard to those standards as a guide to what constitutes lawful conditions of detention.

In the same context one Northern Ireland decision is of interest, the case of *R. v. McCormick*,[14] in which a bolder line was adopted by McConigal LJ. The issue concerned the admissibility of statements made by the accused and the provisions of section 6 of the Northern Ireland (Emergency Provision) Act 1973 which provided that statements were to be admissible unless '*prima facie* evidence

11. *Williams v. Home Office (No.2)* [1981] 1 All ER 1211.

12. *Reg. v. Secretary of State for the Home Department ex p. Herbage* [1987] Q.B. 872.

13. *Weldon v. Home Office* [1992] A.C. 58; the actual decision of the Court of Appeal was reversed by the House of Lords.

14. *Reg. v. McCormick* [1977] N.I. 105.

is adduced that the accused was subjected to torture or inhuman or degrading treatment'. McConigal LJ considered that, in using those words, Parliament was plainly adopting the standards laid down in Article 3 and incorporating them into domestic legislation. He consequently felt free to treat the meaning ascribed to the words by the Convention organs as being at the very least of persuasive value, even if not decisive, and he proceeded to carry out out a careful analysis of the Commission's case-law under Article 3.

B. Development of the Common Law

Here again the courts have shown a perhaps understandable reticence in using the Convention to develop the common law, particularly in a novel or complex field of law. The point was well expressed in the *Malone*[15] case—the telephone tapping case—in which Sir Robert Megarry noted that, where Parliament had abstained from legislating on a point that was plainly suitable for legislation, it was:

> indeed difficult for the court to lay down new rules of common law or equity that will carry out the Crown's treaty obligations or discover for the first time that such rules have always existed.

What is more, as in the case of statutes, when the law is clearly and unambiguously defined in established case law, it is apparent that invocation of the Convention will prove fruitless. This is clear from the case of *In re M. & H. (Minors)*[16] in which the House of Lords rejected an attempt by the appellant to invoke the Convention as the basis for persuading the House of Lords to depart from two previous decisions of its own.

The Convention has nevertheless proved of some limited value in resolving uncertainties in the common law and in pointing the way in which the common law should develop. Two examples in particular are worth mentioning.

First, in the area of contempt of court. With the proliferation of administrative and quasi-judicial tribunals, one of the difficult questions with which the domestic courts have on occasions been faced is whether a particular tribunal is to be treated as a 'court' for the purposes of the law of contempt. In resolving

15. *Malone v. Metropolitan Police Commission* [1979] Ch.344.
16. [1990] 1 A.C. 686.

this question recourse has been had to the Convention. Article 10 of the Convention was invoked by two members of the House of Lords in *A.G. v. B.B.C.*[17] as providing strong support for their view that an extension of the law of contempt to include proceedings in a local valuation court would not be justified: to countenance such an extension so that comment on proceedings pending in a valuation court could be restrained as a contempt would in their view have given rise to an unjustifiable interference with freedom of expression. By contrast in *P. v. Liverpool Post plc*[18] the Court of Appeal relied on Article 5 of the Convention in support of its conclusion that a Mental Health Appeal Tribunal was a court for the purposes of contempt, the argument being that if such a tribunal was not a 'court' for all purposes, Article 5(4) of the Convention, which requires that the lawfulness of a person's detention should be decided speedily 'by a court,' would not be complied with.

Again, Article 6 of the Convention as interpreted by the European Court of Human Rights in the *Golder* case was relied on by the House of Lords in *Raymond v. Honey*[19] as affirming the principle that the denial of access to court by a prisoner was a contempt of court, as being an interference with the due administration of justice. The same principle also played an important part in the reasoning of the Divisional Court in the *Anderson*[20] case, the case in which a challenge was made to the so-called 'simultaneous ventilation' rule whereby prisoners wishing to make a complaint in correspondence about prison treatment were obliged simultaneously to ventilate the complaint internally through a prescribed procedure. The Court held, applying the principle in the *Golder* case, that the rule served as an impediment to a prisoner's right of access to a legal adviser and thereby his right of access to a court and on this ground held the rule to be *ultra vires*.

The second area of the common law which worthy of mention is the law of blasphemy.

In the case of *Reg. v. Lemon*[21] the House of Lords held, *inter alia*, that a blasphemous libel was a publication which was calculated to outrage the feelings of Christians. In a case decided by the Divisional Court last year called

17. [1981] A.C. 303.
18. [1990] 2 W.L.R. 494.
19. [1983] 1 A.C. 1.
20. *Reg. v. Secretary of State for the Home Department ex p. Anderson* [1984] Q.B. 778.
21. [1979] A.C. 617.

Choudhury[22] an attempt was made to persuade the Court that the common law offence was not restricted to the Christian religion but should extend to other religions. The case involved an attempt to prosecute Salman Rushdie and his publishers for blasphemy for the publication of 'The Satanic Verses'.

In support of his argument the applicant sought to rely on the provisions of Article 9 of the Convention—the right to freedom of religion—and Article 14—freedom from discriminatory treatment. A substantial part of the Court's interesting judgment was devoted to a careful analysis of the Convention under the expert guidance of Anthony Lester, who appeared for the respondents. The judgment contained not only a convincing explanation as to why Articles 9 and 14 did not require the extension of a law of blasphemy to include other religions but an equally convincing explanation as to why any such extension would run the risk of violating Articles 7 and 10 of the Convention.

C. *Judicial Review of Administrative Decisions*

It is perhaps here that the scope for invoking the Convention might be thought to be greatest. Certainly there was a promising start: in *Bhajan Singh* Lord Denning held that not only were the courts bound to take the Convention into account whenever interpreting a statute affecting the rights and liberties of the individual, but that immigration officers and the Secretary of State were also required to bear in mind the principles stated in the Convention when exercising their decision-making functions.

This view was short-lived. In the following year in the *Bibi* case Lord Denning again recanted, stating that it would be too much to expect immigration officers to know or to apply the Convention.

The same approach was adopted by the Court of Appeal in the *Fernandes*[23] case in 1980 in which the Court held that there was no legal obligation on the Secretary of State to consider whether or not a particular course of action would contravene the Convention.

In the 10–year period between the *Fernandes* case and the cases of *Brind* and *Colman* the authorities contain very little discussion of the Convention in the context of challenges to administrative decisions. However, two decisions may be of some interest.

22. Reg. v. Chief Metropolitan Stipendiary Magistrate ex p. Chandbury [1991] 1 Q.B. 429.
23. *Fernandes v. Secretary of State for the Home Department,* [1981] Imm. A.R.1.

The first is the case of *McAvoy*[24] in which the Court held that, in deciding to transfer a prisoner from one prison to another, the Secretary of State was obliged to have regard to two rights enjoyed by an unconvicted prisoner: the right to visits from his family and the right to visits from his solicitor and, thereby, the right of access to a court and the right to a fair trial. The Court accepted that these were not what were described in the judgment as 'traditional common law rights' and that they were not rights which were conferred in terms by the Prison Act or the Prison Rules. They were to be found, if anywhere, in Articles 8 and 6 of the Convention. Without deciding whether these Convention rights were in themselves justiciable, the Court felt able to say that these rights were reflected in the provisions of the Prison Rules and thus were matters to which the Secretary of State was bound to have regard.

The other case is the House of Lords case of *Hone and McCartan*[25] decided in 1988. The only issue raised in the appeal to the House of Lords was whether a prisoner appearing before a Board of Visitors was entitled as of right to legal representation at the hearing. The House answered the question in the negative, approving the decision of the Divisional Court in *Tarrant*[26] to the effect that the question whether legal representation should be allowed was a matter of discretion. In so doing the House examined the jurisprudence of the European Court of Human Rights in the *Engel* case and in the case of *Campbell and Fell* for the purpose of determining whether any such absolute right to representation existed under the Convention. The House concluded that it did not. More importantly perhaps, it concluded that the factors which the Convention organs took into account in determining whether particular disciplinary proceedings fell within Article 6 at all (namely, the seriousness of the offence and the severity of the possible penalty) were precisely the same factors to which the Board of Visitors would be required to have regard in the exercise of their discretion.

I turn finally to the case of *Brind*. There would seem to be three principle strands in the reasoning of the House.

First, it is clearly established that the presumption, which applies in a case of ambiguity or uncertainty, that Parliament intended to legislate in conformity with the Convention cannot be applied by analogy to the exercise of a statutory

24. *Reg. v. Secretary of State for the Home Department, ex p. McAvoy* [1984] 1 W.L.R. 1408.

25. *Reg. v. Board of Visitors of H.M. Prison, The Maze, ex p. Hone and McCartan* [1988] A.C. 379.

26. *Reg. v. Secretary of State for the Home Department ex p. Tarrant* [1985] Q.B. 251.

discretion. To apply such a presumption would be, to use the words of Lord Bridge:

> to go far beyond the resolution of an ambiguity. It would be to impute to Parliament an intention not only that the executive should exercise the discretion in conformity with the Convention, but also that the domestic courts should enforce that conformity by the importation into domestic administrative law of the text of the Convention and the jurisprudence of the European Court of Human Rights in the interpretation and application of it.

In the view of the Lords this would in effect be to incorporate the Convention into an important area of domestic law and would be a judicial usurpation of the legislative functions.

Secondly, however, this did **not** mean that the courts were powerless to prevent the exercise by the executive of administrative discretion, even a discretion conferred in unlimited terms, in a way which infringed fundamental human rights. The courts were entitled to start from the premise that any restriction of the right to freedom of expression (or presumably any other Convention right) required to be justified and that nothing less than an important competing public interest would be sufficient to justify it. The primary judgment fell to be made by the Secretary of State. But the courts were entitled to exercise a secondary judgment in accordance with *Wednesbury* principles by asking whether a reasonable Secretary of State, on the material before him, could reasonably make that primary judgment.

Thirdly, the principle of 'proportionality', which is recognised in the administrative law of several member states of the EEC and to which reference was made by Lord Diplock in the *G.C.H.Q.* case, did not yet form part of our administrative law and could not be applied in the present case, since to do so would be for the court to substitute its own judgment for that of the Secretary of State.

It is the second strand which appears to me to be the most important for present purposes. The Lords held that,on the particular facts of the *Brind* case, the interference complained of was minimal and the reasons given by the Secretary of State for imposing the broadcasting ban were compelling. For this reason the Lords had no hesitation in holding that the Secretary of State had not exceeded the limits of his discretion and that his decision to impose the ban was not 'irrational' according to *Wednesbury* principles.

But the significance of the decision is the apparent recognition in the judgments of three of their Lordships—Lord Bridge, Lord Roskill and Lord Templeman—that an executive decision which restricts or interferes with fundamental rights and freedoms may be treated by the domestic courts as 'irrational' unless the decision maker could reasonably conclude on the material before him that the particular restriction was justified by a competing public interest or, to use the words of Lord Templeman, that the interference was 'necessary and proportionate to the damage which the restriction is designed to prevent'.

If this is the correct interpretation of the judgments, which the author does not find altogether easy, it is clearly a decision of some considerable potential importance: even if this interpretation is correct, the precise limits of the principle would have to be worked out. In particular, what would an applicant have to show in order to satisfy the court that a decision was irrational? Presumably he would have to do more than show that the decision would or was likely to involve a breach of the Convention, otherwise this would be tantamount to the judicial incorporation of the Convention which the House of Lords regarded as unacceptable. On the other hand, if the applicant were required to show that no reasonable Minister could ever have concluded, on the basis of the material before him, that the restriction or interference was justified in terms of the Convention, the burden is likely to prove difficult if not impossible to discharge.

The record of the domestic courts in addressing the Convention and in their treatment of Convention issues has been patchy. This is perhaps inevitable in view of the concern of the courts not to usurp the function of Parliament and not to be seen to be admitting the Convention by the back door, where the legislature has refused it admission by the front. Nevertheless, even within these obvious limitations, there have been positive and welcome developments in which imaginative use has been made by the courts of the Convention, particularly in the area of prisons and prisoners' rights. There still remains ample scope in my view for a bolder use of the Convention both in the development of the common law and in the review of administrative decisions. Although in the result the *Brind* case is hardly promising, it may provide at least a basis for a more imaginative judicial approach in the future. This would be a welcome development.

Chapter 7

CHILDREN IN CARE AND THE EUROPEAN CONVENTION ON HUMAN RIGHTS

Françoise J. Hampson

I. INTRODUCTION

THIS paper deals with a specific situation—children in the care of a local authority and not therefore with the protection of private and family life against invasions by other individuals. In terms of the European Convention on Human Rights, the obligation of the State to protect individuals from the actions of third parties seems to be more limited than its obligation itself not to violate the right in question. In the case of children in care, we are dealing with individuals in the care of the State. It therefore involves the obligation of the State not itself to violate the rights applicable. Since the obligation is more onerous, we might expect there to be a greater risk of violation. I have proposed elsewhere[1] that the case-law suggests that, relatively speaking, the United Kingdom's track record is quite good when it comes to balancing the competing rights of individuals but that its record is less good where the dispute is between an individual and an authority for which the State is responsible. In the fields of prisoners, mental health detainees, persons seeking entry to the United Kingdom, the right of detainees to be brought promptly before a judge, the United Kingdom has been found in violation of the Convention. This suggests a particular problem in how the United Kingdom deals with those being looked after by the State. In that

1. F.J. Hampson, 'The United Kingdom before the European Court of Human Rights', 9 Yearbook of European Law (1989) 121. I would like to thank my colleague Kate Standley for her help in identifying and clarifying the provisions of domestic law and for commenting on a draft of this note. Any errors and the oversimplifications are entirely my responsibility.

case, one would expect to find problems in the State's treatment of children in its care. There are therefore two factors, the one general and the other particular to the United Kingdom, which suggest a predisposition to breach the Convention in situations such as that being considered here. Is that in fact the case and, if so, why?

II. THE LEGAL REGIMES

THIS paper does not deal with adoption, disputes between parents where the child is in the care of one of them or the position in Scotland. An initial problem is that the regime applicable to children in care has undergone three dramatic changes in the past ten years. The first system was that which applied in the case of *O. v. U.K.*, *H. v. U.K.*, *W. v. U.K.*, *B. v. U.K.* and *R. v. U.K.*[2] These will be referred to as the *Alphabet* cases. Whilst those cases were before the Commission, changes were introduced into the Child Care Act 1980 by means of the Health and Social Services and Social Security Adjudications Act 1983. The third regime was that introduced by the Children Act 1989, which came into force in October 1991. This Act represents a fundamental and comprehensive overhaul of the whole question of the care of children, not just those in care, and is based on a completely different philosophy from that which prevailed previously. It is the product of problems revealed by cases such as that of Jasmine Beckford, the victim of abuse at the hands of her parents, the problems which were revealed in the system itself by groups of cases such as the Cleveland and Shetland affairs, allegations of serious ill-treatment of children in care and the continuing difficulties in reconciling the child's rights, the parents' rights and the best interests of the child which the local authority claims to represent. These difficulties often centre round the question of access to the child in care.

III. THE ISSUES

THE issues which arise include:

1. The taking of children into care—on what grounds and in what circumstances can that happen?

2. *O. and H. v. U.K.*,ECHR, Series A, No. 120; *W, B and R. v. U.K.*, ECHR, Series A, No.121.

2. The manner in which the child is taken into care.
3. The treatment the child receives whilst in care.
4. The right of the parents—to be consulted.
5. The right of the parents—to access.
6. The best interests of the child. Who should decide what they are?

These in turn raise issues of more general concern, such as:

7. The degree to which the child should be consulted.
8. Mechanisms enabling children to complain of treatment at the hands of their parents and in care.
9. The child's capacity to bring legal actions.
10. The problems posed by evidence of children in criminal and civil proceedings.

These cut across the different stages in the process: when is a child taken into care, how is a child taken into care and how is the child in care treated.

This paper does not attempt even to consider the more general problems, which arise on account of the child's status as a minor. They are not peculiar to the child care system. Nevertheless, it is emphasised that, as human rights issues, they are important. In particular, the legal capacity of a child and the weight to be attached to the evidence of a child, whether in criminal or civil proceedings, seem to be matters of some importance. However, this paper focuses on problems peculiar to the care situation.

IV. ON WHAT GROUNDS CAN CHILDREN BE TAKEN INTO CARE

A. Voluntarily

Where parents could not care for a child, usually for reasons of a temporary nature, such as illness, the parent could voluntarily place the child in care. If it appeared to the local authority that certain grounds were proved, the local authority was under a duty to receive the child into care. Under the new system, voluntary placement does not appear to come within the provisions of the Act on care orders. Under s.8, any order can be sought if necessary. A child who has voluntarily been placed in the care of a local authority may subsequently, whilst in care, be the object of a care order.

B. *Involuntarily*

Of more significance, not least because it is more likely to lead to disputes, is the compulsory taking of children into care. In the past, one way in which a child could come into care was by the application of the local authority to the Juvenile Court for a care order under s.1 of the Children and Young Persons Act 1969. The order could be made where the child's proper development was being avoidably prevented or neglected or on the grounds of health or ill-treatment or because the child was in need of care and control. The child could also be placed in care as a result of wardship proceedings.

Under the new Act, there is a different system. The changes in some areas, and this is one of them, may be more apparent than real. It is too soon to say. The philosophy, however, is completely different and that may have a knock-on effect on how the changes work in practice. It is necessary to outline that underlying philosophy because it explains so much about the Children Act. First, it is recognised that there may be a distinction between parenthood, which attaches permanently to the natural parents of the child, and parental responsibility which attaches to those exercising care and control. Severing the interests, as it were, enables the law to recognise continuing content in the parent-child relationship. Rights or responsibilities are not exclusive. Different 'rights' may exist concurrently. This could be useful in some cases under Article 8 of the European Convention on Human Rights, where the government denies the existence of 'family life', or under Article 6 where it claims that no right is at issue.

Then there is the role of the court which, under the Act, has been changed fundamentally. In certain areas, the court will itself take decisions which were formerly the preserve of the local authority. In the past, the local authority took decisions in relation to which, in most cases, only judicial review was available. Not only was that subject to the notorious limitations of such proceedings but the Court of Appeal[3] had told the Juvenile Courts to exercise their powers with great restraint, on account of the risk of disturbing the local authority's plans for the child. In certain of the alphabet cases, the lack of independent and impartial proceedings to resolve disputes was held to be a breach of Article 6 of the Convention. To the extent to which the new Act gives the Court the power to make the initial determination, this would appear to reduce the scope for

3. *Re M (a Minor)(Access Application)*, [1988] 1 FLR 35 at 38.

complaints under that Article. It remains to be seen whether the results will be any different.

This philosophy goes hand in hand with another remarkable provision. Under s.1(5) of the Children Act, where a court is considering whether or not to make one or more orders under this Act with respect to a child, it shall not make the orders unless it considers that doing so would be better for the child than making no order. We shall return to this in a moment. The comprehensiveness of the new code is also demonstrated by the removal of most of the wardship powers of the local authority.

On what grounds them, under the new Act, can a child be taken into care? S.31 provides that a court can only make a care order or supervision order on the application of a local authority if:

(a) the child is suffering or likely to suffer significant harm; and
(b) the harm or likelihood of it is attributable to:
  (i) the care given to the child if the order were not made, not being what it would be reasonable to expect the parent to give him; or
  (ii) the child's being beyond parental control.

Most of the terms are defined in the section. It will be noted that it is possible for an authority to seek an order on the strength of *apprehended* harm in the case of children already born. This is an innovation and litigation is likely over any such determinations.

Even where the statutory minimum conditions of s.31 are satisfied, the court will then apply s.1, which requires it to have the child's welfare as the paramount consideration, to take into account seven specific considerations and which also requires the court to conclude that some order is better than none. The grounds in s.31 are therefore necessary but not, of themselves, sufficient to justify the decision.

The order can be made during the course of any 'family proceedings', both private or public, and not just in proceedings brought for the purpose. The effect of a care order is defined for the first time in s.33. In particular, the local authority acquires parental responsibility for the child and has the power to determine the extent to which a parent can meet his/her parental responsibilities. The local authority cannot, however, change the child's religion or consent to the adoption of the child. The local authority is required to consult the parents and the child and other relevant persons before taking a decision about the child. It has to give due consideration to listed factors. That could lead to legal challenges.

How are the new grounds likely to fare before the European Commission and Court of Human Rights? It should first be noted that the *grounds* for taking into care do not usually pose a problem. No Western European State takes children into care unless it claims to believe that it is in the child's best interests. The problems usually concern the application of those grounds on the facts. Under the new Act, the parents can contest an application by the local authority. The child's views are not one of the factors to be taken into account. There is a timetable in s.32 for disposing of applications for orders. Given the reluctance of the Commission to challenge the sufficiency of the grounds for taking into care, as opposed to the procedure used, it would seem that the new Act should avoid many potential problems for the United Kingdom The most likely exception would be the new ground of *apprehended* harm.

V. TREATMENT OF THE CHILD IN CARE

THE procedure used to take children into care could raise issues under Article 8 and, in extreme cases, Article 3 of the European Convention on Human Rights. Press reports of the Shetland case, for example, suggest that children were woken up and taken away in the middle of the night, without the time for any parental reassurance, even under supervision, and not even allowed to take a familiar toy with them. If true, this would appear to raise issues under Article 8 in relation to both the parents and the children and possibly under Article 3 (inhuman treatment) in relation to the children. Such cases are much more likely to depend on the facts than on the law. The need for prompt and unannounced action can arise in a variety of situations. That does not, however, justify causing additional and unnecessary suffering to the children concerned.

VI. TREATMENT OF THE CHILD IN CARE

THE local authority has the duty of safeguarding and promoting the welfare of the child. Where the treatment of the child in care is unacceptable, the child will have the normal common-law remedies for ill-treatment. Access to those remedies may pose difficulties. It is not clear whether an action for breach of statutory duty would lie or whether an order could be sought under the Act. The court is to appoint a *guardian ad litem* in defined proceedings, unless that is not necessary in order to safeguard the child's interest. That does, however, require that the issue has already reached the courts. Every local authority is also required under s.26(3) to establish a procedure for considering representations and complaints, including those of a child. One problem may be the British acceptance of measures against children which would not be used against adults: the question of corporal punishment springs to mind. The use of the 'pin-down' system might also raise difficulties under the Convention.

VII. PARENTAL ACCESS TO CHILDREN IN CARE

THIS used to be perhaps the biggest bone of contention. Under the regime before the Children Act, except in cases of wardship, access arrangements were determined by the local authority. If the arrangements were to be terminated or the authority refused to make any arrangements, the parent had to be notified and told of his/her right to apply to the juvenile court for an access order, with appeal to the High Court. The right to seek an access order did not apply to changes short of termination. Nor did it enable the parent to challenge the arrangements themselves. There was however a Code of Practice which provided that in most cases the aim was to secure the eventual reunification of the family (which may satisfy the test the European Court of Human Rights appeared to adopt in the *Olsson Case*).[4] To that end, parents were to be involved in the planning of the care of the child, including the access arrangements. The Code of Practice was not generally regarded as legally enforceable.

The Children Act, in para.15 of Schedule 2, requires the local authority to endeavour to promote contact between the child and his parents, unless it is not reasonably practicable or consistent with his welfare. S.34 of the Act itself requires the local authority to allow the child reasonable contact with his parents, unless it is necessary to refuse contact to safe-guard or promote the child's welfare. In that case, it can refuse contact for not more than seven days, after which time the local authority must have obtained a court order. A parent or the authority or the child can apply to the court for an access order and the *court* may make such order as it considers appropriate. In other words, the decision is that of the court.

4. *Olsson v. Sweden*, ECHR, Series A, No.130.

What makes this so striking a change is that, in the case of *W. v. U.K.*, the government was concerned that the question should not be removed from the discretion of the local authority and the Court indicated a certain sympathy with the concern. The British government is now prepared to leave the decision itself, and not merely a power of review, to a court.

VIII. THE COURTS AND THE CHILDREN ACT

THIS raises the issue of how the courts will handle the Children Act. If the Act itself seems to have addressed many of the concerns in the alphabet cases, this does not mean that the application of the Act will keep the United Kingdom out of the Commission and Court. The application in practice depends in part on social workers and in part on the courts. Insofar as the courts are reluctant to review the decisions of the local authority, which they certainly were under the old system, a heavy burden is placed on social workers, whom the Secretary of State is currently drowning in a sea of directions and regulations. In certain areas, as we have seen, the decision is to be taken by the court. The courts have therefore both a primary and a secondary responsibility under the Children Act. What does the attitude of the courts in relation to the old legislation tell us about its likely attitude to decisions under the new Act?

A note of caution should be sounded—judges are supposed to have received special training, in preparation for the entry into force of the new Act, from lawyers, officials and social workers. If they understand what the Act is trying to do, they may depart from previously held attitudes. Such a change of attitude is not only desirable but also necessary if the philosophy of the Act is not to be totally undermined and if the United Kingdom is not to find itself before the Commission and Court again.

It will be recalled that under the old system there was a non-binding Code of Practice which sought to promote consultation and recognised the importance of continuing contact between parent and child. Furthermore, as a matter of law, the court was required to use the criterion of the best interests of the child as the first and paramount concern. This might be thought to imply that there were other considerations which might be relevant, such as the right of the parent or the notion that contact with parents would generally be in the best interests of the child. That was not, however, reflected in the case-law. In *Hereford &*

Worcester Country Council v. JAH,[5] the court held that the paramount concern for the best interests of the child should not be 'influenced by the conception that the natural parent has a right to that access to the child. That right is a right which is the product of the court's decision'. In other words, it is not seen as inherent in the parent-child relationship. In *Coventry City Council v. T*,[6] the court held that 'consideration of the natural parents' deep feelings for the child is totally irrelevant to the question of access unless it can be shown that access would be beneficial to the child'. In other words, it was not enough to show a lack of harm, it was necessary to prove positive benefit. This is in contrast to the notion that, in general, contact is in the best interests of the child. It is also in conflict with the Commission's case-law. The Commission stated, in *L. v. Sweden*, that 'Under Article 8, an interference with the right of the parents to continue to take care of their child cannot be justified simply on the basis that it would be better for the child to be taken care of by certain foster parents. In order to justify such an interference it is necessary under the terms of Article 8 that the State demonstrates sufficient reason for the decision to take a child into care'.[7]

Applying this reasoning to access, it is not up to the parent to establish that the child would benefit from access.

Why are English judges so reluctant to attach the requisite weight to the parents' interest? I would suggest that a possible explanation is to be found in the judgment of Lord Oliver in *Re K.D. (A Minor) (Ward: Termination of Access)*.[8] Having said that any perceived conflict between the 'welfare principle' and the parental right of access was purely semantic, he continued, 'Counsel for the appellant ... invites your Lordships to accept and pronounce that the starting point in every case should be that a parent has a right of access which should be given effect to by the court and curtailed and inhibited only if the court is satisfied that the exercise of the right will be positively inimical to the interests of the child'.[9] Now you might think that that was not only common sense but also the intention of the combination of the statute and the Code of Practice and consistent with

5. [1985] FLR 530 at 533-534.
6. [1986] 2 FLR 301 at 305, cited in *Re M (a Minor)(Access Application)*, [1988] 1 FLR 35 at 38.
7. 40 D&R 140 at 151-152.
8. [1988] 1 All ER 577.
9. Ibid at 590.

Article 8 of the European Convention on Human Rights. Lord Oliver concluded, 'My Lords, for my part, I think that this is an invitation which your Lordships should decline'.[10]

It is too soon to say how judges will handle the Children Act. Lord Oliver's words, however, do not bode well for decisions under the new Act.[11] In that case, the European Commission and Court of Human Rights have not seen the last of cases dealing with children in the care of local authorities in England and Wales.

10. Ibid.

11. As emphasised above, decisions on access are no longer executive determinations but matters for the court. There is now a **duty** to promote access. The issue of access does not, so far, appear to have caused problems under the new law. When it comes to the judicial attitude to the philosophy underlying the Act, however, there is cause for concern arising out of decisions in other areas. For example, children are supposed to be able to bring applications in their own right. Under s.8 of the Act, a child needs leave to do so. Under a practice direction, the leave of the **High Court** must be obtained. If the court grants leave, it is likely to order that the child be represented by the Official Solicitor, rather than by the child's own solicitor. This may reintroduce wardship by the back door. In practice, the court is not likely to disagree with the conclusions of a *guardian ad litem*. My thanks to Carolyn Hamilton for commenting on the operation of the Act in practice.

Chapter 8

PROCEDURAL INCORPORATION: THE RIGHT TO REMEDIES

J.P. Gardner

THE European Convention on Human Rights constitutes a milestone in the international protection of human rights. This description is appropriate because the Convention provides an effective system for the protection of Human Rights and has served as a model for other systems.

The purpose of the present collection of papers is not to examine the operation of the Convention system in isolation, nor to compare it with other systems for the international protection of fundamental rights. The object is to relate the Convention to domestic law, to examine its relevance and the legal issues which its incorporation into domestic law gives rise to.

As a common lawyer, I propose to tackle one aspect of this question from a common lawyer's perspective. As a result I will not examine whether, if fundamental rights norms are adopted into municipal law, they should be the rights of Part I of the Convention or other rights[1].

The reason for this is simple. Common lawyers are interested in remedies, not rights, and so it is on the Convention's remedies that I will concentrate. This approach also reflects the contention that the Convention system is effective. Effectiveness involves an assessment of the practical consequences of proceedings in any given case[2] and also an assessment of the effectiveness of the procedure itself. This assessment can again be subdivided between potential and actual effectiveness. The Convention machinery acquits itself well on the first of these

1. For convincing arguments why the Convention is the most sensible choice, see House of Lords Select Committee on the European Communities, 71st Report 1979-80, HL362 and 1993, 3rd Report 1992/3 HL10.

2. See Chapter 9 *infra* Churchill.

two assessments: the availability of individual petition, the absence of procedural formality and the special role of the Commission before the Court were all features intended to ensure the effectiveness of the Convention system from its inception.

Practical effectiveness is less easy to be confident about. The sheer number of applications lodged now overburdens a system which has at last attained the generalised acceptance of the right of individual petition and of the jurisdiction of the Court[3]. The hybrid nature of the Commission's role, as quasi-judicial instance and *amicus curiae* before the Court, has been replaced in practice by a huge development of case-law on admissibility by the Commission and the overhaul of the place of individuals before the Court[4].

Most significantly, however, has been the development of the doctrine of effectiveness in the case-law of, first, the Court[5] and subsequently the Commission. This case-law has not only greatly increased the scope of application of the Convention[6], but has placed the emphasis of that development on procedural rather than substantive rights - the right to remedies.

The Convention provides one remedy for individuals - or, in continental terms, protects one right, and that is optional[7]. It is the right for

> any person, non-governmental organisation or group of individuals claiming to be a victim of a violation by one of the High Contracting Parties of the rights set forth in this Convention . . .

to lodge a petition with the Commission.[8] Articles 26–28 provide that the

3. As at 1 May 1993 26 States have ratified the Convention and all have accepted Article 25 and the jurisdiction of the Court (Article 46). By comparison, in 1980 of twenty States Party, fourteen had accepted Article 25.

4. Revised Rules of Court of 24 November 1982 and the major reform introduced by Protocol 9 granting individuals the opportunity to refer cases to the Court.

5. E.g. *Klass* case judgment of 18 November 1977 Series A, Vol. 28, para. 34.

6. Some striking examples are:- case of *Le Compte Van Leuven and De Meyere*, judgment of 23 June 1981, Series A, Vol. 43. Case of *Minelli* judgment of 25 March 1983 Series A, Vol. 62. *Olsson v Sweden*, Com. Rap. 1.12.86, paras. 153-178 in Series A, Vol. 130, pps. 56-62. *Bramelid and Malmström v Sweden*, Com. Rap. 12.12.83. DR 38 p.18.

7. See fn.3 *supra*. Poland and Hungary were admitted to the Council of Europe without ratifying the Convention until after a law reform process had been completed. The acceptance of Articles 25(1) and 46 is now a matter of political fact for Member States of the Council of Europe which may amount to a binding practice.

8. Article 25(1).

Commission must then decide upon the admissibility of that complaint.

In the majority of cases this involves the Commission, and later the Court, in examining whether the Convention has been breached taking account of an individual's particular circumstances. For example, whether a trial has been fair,[9] or whether ban on a demonstration was necessary.[10]

Cases of that kind raise the question whether the individual has a remedy under the Convention for the breach of their right. If the individual chooses to complain[11], the Commission *must* consider the matter[12]. In this respect the Convention procedure is essentially similar to domestic civil litigation. There is a plaintiff who seeks redress for a particular wrong.

The wrong is not usually one which sounds in damages, it is of a special kind – a fundamental right. Usually the proceedings should be classified as public or administrative law proceedings. The concept of the rule of law dictates that the prime concern in such cases will be to ensure that the law is observed, and that unlawful action is prohibited or stopped, rather than to award damages[13]. Nevertheless the similarity of the Strasbourg procedure to domestic litigation makes it natural that lawyers seeking remedies think in terms of incorporating the Convention, so that the remedies can be sought before the domestic courts.

Whatever the merits and demerits of that debate as it affects decisions on an individual's particular circumstances, the present paper concentrates on the other kind of individual case, where the Commission and the Court perform a different role. This category concerns cases where a remedy is sought in Strasbourg against the state of domestic law, rather than to remedy one specific incident. What is at stake is the review of legislation[14] for conformity with the Conven-

9. Article 6; *Barberà Messegué and Jabardo* case, judgment of 6 December 1988, Series A, Vol. 146.

10. Article 11; *Plattform 'Ärtze für das Leben'* case, judgment of 21 June 1988 Series A, Vol. 139.

11. It has been crucial to the Commission's progressive development as a first instance jurisdiction that it has no power to initiate an investigation into possible human rights 'situations'.

12. The obligatory nature of the Commission's jurisdiction once an application is lodged is characteristic of a petition-based remedy system under international law. It contrasts starkly with the discretionary jurisdiction of national supreme courts with which the Commission and the Court are frequently compared.

13. Compare the limited availability of damages for constitutional wrongs in domestic jurisdictions, e.g. *Edelman v Jordan* 415 US 651 (1974); *Prat-Flottes Conseil d'Etat* CE 15 juillet 1964; BGH 13.12.1965, BGHZ 45, 143 [146].

14. Or, more correctly, the state of domestic law.

tion. I will seek to argue that this aspect of petitions under the Convention represents the greatest constitutional challenge, not only for this country, but for the majority of Member States of the Council of Europe.

I will start by illustrating this special role from the Strasbourg cases. This part will identify some of the special issues to which this review gives rise; reference will then be made to the availability of judicial review of legislation in the domestic law of some Council of Europe jurisdictions. Finally, I shall draw some conclusions as to the implications of the incorporation of this jurisdiction into English law for the law of remedies.

I. REVIEW OF LEGISLATION BY THE COMMISSION AND COURT

FORMALLY, the Commission and the Court do not review legislation *in abstracto*: the victim requirement of Article 25(1) prevents this.[15] In a number of cases, however, the Commission and Court have accepted an applicant as a victim without much of a conscience. This has been especially so in those cases where the Convention has been read to impose a 'positive obligation'.

In the *Marckx* case,[16] an unmarried mother and her daughter complained about their legal relationship under Belgian law. Belgian law required the mother to take formal steps to establish her legal relationship with her daughter. Mother and daughter argued that this failed to show 'respect for family life'[17] and that the differences between the daughter's legal status and that of a child born to married parents was discriminatory. They won.

The Court held that the applicants did not need to show detriment to themselves in order to claim to be victims of a breach of their rights under Article 8.

15. For an analysis of this doctrine see K. Rogge, 'The victim requirement in Article 25 of the European Convention on Human Rights' in Matscher and Petzold (Eds.) *Protecting Human Rights: the European Dimension* Carl Heymanns Verlag (1990) p.539 ff.

16. Judgment of 13 June 1979, Series A, Vol.31.

17. The positive obligation on States which the Court has interpreted from Article 8 derives particularly from the opening words of the text: '*Everyone has the right to respect for . . . Toute personne a droit au respect de . . .*'. The text does not guarantee a right to family life, but see No. 7922/77 Dec. 12.12.77 DR 12 p.192, No. 8427/78, Rap. Com. 13.3.1980, DR18 p.225 and *Olsson* case, *supra* n.6.

> Article 25 of the Convention entitles individuals to contend that a law violates their rights by itself in the absence of an individual measure of implementation if they run the risk of being directly affected by it.[18]

The Court's jurisdiction derived from the fact that the applicants 'challenged a legal position - that of unmarried mothers and of children born out of wedlock - which affected them personally'.

The Commission's approach to this question of *locus standi* was clearer still in the Danish sex education case, *Kjeldsen, Busk Madsen and Pedersen*[19]. The applicants complained as parents that compulsory sex education introduced by an Act of 1970 was contrary to their philosophical convictions[20]. They objected first to the Act and secondly to the official directives issued to schools about how sex education should be carried out.

The Commission rejected the latter complaints for failure to exhaust domestic remedies, but accepted the complaint about the legislation. On the merits it tied 7 to 7 (with the President's casting vote for no violation) as to whether the mere existence of the sex education system was a breach of the Convention. The Court reached the same conclusion on the merits, but in so doing stated[21]

> The Court is called upon to ascertain whether or not the Act and the delegated legislation thereunder contravenes the Convention.

In carrying out this assessment the Court concluded that the legislation[22]

> . . . did not involve overstepping the bounds of what a democratic State may regard as the public interest.

The question of the review of legislation for conformity with the Convention has also arisen in prominent cases against the United Kingdom concerning the criminalisation of homosexuality in Northern Ireland,[23] leasehold reform legislation[24] and the Aircraft and Shipbuilding Industries Act 1977.[25]

18. *Marckx* case n.16 *supra* para. 27.
19. Application Nos. 5095/71, 5920/72 and 5926/72, Rap.Comm. 21.3.75.
20. Article 2, Protocol No.1 protects the right of parents to ensure that their children's education and teaching is in conformity with their own religious and philosophical convictions.
21. Judgment of 7 December 1976, Series A, Vol.23, para.48.
22. *Ibid* para. 54.
23. *Dudgeon* case judgment of 22 October 1981 Series A, Vol. 45.
24. *James and Others* case judgment of 21 February 1986 Series A, Vol. 98.

The different approaches adopted in each of these cases serve to underline the Court's difficulty of resolving *locus standi* on the one hand and the jurisdiction to review legislation on the other. In *Dudgeon* the Court adopted a very similar approach to that in *Marckx* stating that 'the very existence of this legislation continuously and directly affects (the applicant's) private life'.[26] As a result, the Court reviewed the justification for the Offences Against the Person Act 1861 and the Criminal Law Amendment Act 1885, and in so doing was faced with the Government's statement to Parliament abandoning the proposed reform of the law in the face of a substantial body of opinion in Northern Ireland opposed to a change in the law.[27]

In the *James and Others* case concerned with leasehold enfranchisement, the applicants, the trustees of the Duke of Westminster's Estate, complained of each enfranchisement transaction under the Leasehold Reform Act 1967 and submitted that the merits of each transaction should be examined for conformity with Article 1 Protocol No. 1 to the Convention.

The Commission rejected this approach. It considered that the question whether the applicants' rights under the Convention were breached by the tenants' rights to require enfranchisement had to be determined by considering whether the legislation was compatible with the Convention rather than by separate examination of individual transactions.[28] The United Kingdom Government supported this view.

The Court also adopted this approach although expressing the hesitation that 'it must in proceedings originating in an individual application, confine its attention, as far as possible, to the concrete case'.[29] The Court's subsequent review involved an assessment of whether the legislative choices which had been made were 'irrational or inappropriate'[30] or resulted in placing an excessive burden on the applicants.[31]

The Commission adopted a similar approach in the nationalisation cases of

25. Case of *Lithgow and Others* judgment of 8 July 1986 Series A, Vol. 102.

26. *Dudgeon* case n. 23 *supra* para. 41.

27. Statement of the Secretary of State for Northern Ireland to the House of Commons on 2 July 1979 (quoted *ibid* at para. 26).

28. Rap. Comm. 11.5.84, para. 92, quoted in *James and Others* case (n. 24 *supra*) at p.55.

29. *Ibid* para. 36. In fact the Court referred only briefly to the particular transactions on which the applicants relied to show the leasehold reform legislation to be unfair (*ibid* paras. 57 and 69).

30. *Ibid* para. 68.

31. *Ibid* para. 69.

concentrating its review on the conformity of the compensation system established by the legislation with the Convention rather than, as the applicants contended, examining the consequences of applying that system. Again the respondent Government favoured the Commission's approach but the Court, recalling again the jurisdictional consequences of examining a group of individual applications, considered that it must examine both the legislation and the effects of the legislation 'in the context of the terms and conditions which Parliament had to determine in advance and which had to be of general application to the nationalised companies'.[32]

The difficulty which the Court identified in both these cases of avoiding an *in abstracto* review of legislation by seeking to limit its review to the acts of a given case has arisen in other areas and underlines an appreciation by the Court of the difficulties of assuming a role as a 'European Constitutional Court'. The recent case law developing the interpretation and application of the presumption of innocence in Article 6(2) of the Convention is one example. The Commission's rather narrow approach to the application of Article 6(2) was disapproved and substantially widened by the Court in the *Minelli* case[33] which appeared to establish a general principle. Subsequent cases in which the Commission appeared to apply the principle of *Minelli* underline[34], however, that the Court prefers where possible to emphasise the need to examine the particular facts of the given case as the basis for its decisions.

This emphasis on the individual facts of the case has inevitably undermined the Court's ability to state general rules of interpretation[35] whether for application by the Commission or by the national courts and it is to the consequences of the judgments of the court in domestic law that reference will now be made.

II. ISSUES ARISING FROM THE REVIEW OF LEGISLATION BY THE COURT

32. Case of *Lithgow and Others* n. 25 *supra* paras. 123-124.

33. *Minelli* case judgment of 25 March 1983 Series A, No. 62, para. 34.

34. *Lutz, Englert and Nölkenbockhoff* cases, judgment of 25 August 1987, Series A Vol. 123, *Salabiaku* judgment of 7 October 1988 Series A, Vol. 141.

35. This is clearest in the series of cases on the question what constitutes a 'civil right or obligation' under Art. 6(1), e.g. *Bentham* case, judgment of 23 October 1985 Series A, Vol. 97, para. 35. Compare the majority minority concurring and separate opinions of the Commission quoted *ibid* at pps. 23-43.

WHERE the Commission and the Court have applied a 'constitutional' control to national law to establish whether it is in conformity with the Convention, several consequential questions arise within the domestic legal order.[36] The first is, what is the effect of a finding that legislation is contrary to the Convention?

The Court, under attack from the Belgian Government in the *Marckx* case, asserted that as a matter of Convention law, its judgment was merely declaratory.[37] It retreated behind the doctrine, in accordance with Article 53 of the Convention, that it is for the States to decide upon the means chosen for compliance with a judgment.

This description may be adequate in a State like the United Kingdom where the Convention is not incorporated into domestic law, but is hardly convincing in jurisdictions where the Convention is part of the domestic legal order. In these jurisdictions at least, a distinction must be made between a judgment which is declaratory of the rights of an individual *vis à vis* the State complained against (declaratory therefore of an obligation in international law)[38] and one which is declaratory of the legal rule in the Convention, which is therefore of general application in all those States in which the Convention is incorporated into domestic law.

An example of the latter was the Court's finding of a violation of the right in Article 6(3)(e) in the case of *Luedicke Belkacem and Koç*,[39] where those applicants had been charged for the costs of interpretation in accordance with Article 464(a) paragraph 1 of the German Code of Criminal Procedure. The Court held that the application of that provision to the applicants had resulted in a violation of their rights, but this provision of the Code of Criminal Procedure did not allow for any other result. In consequence, the judgment effectively challenged the domestic legislation which was subsequently amended.[40]

A second question is the effect of a judgment of the Court on third parties in a jurisdiction where the Convention is incorporated. This issue also arose in the *Marckx* case.[41] The Court argued that the effect of its judgment on third parties

36. See also Chapter 4 Nørgaard *supra* on the Danish legislative response to judgments of the Court against Denmark and other States.

37. *Marckx* case n. 16 *supra* para. 58.

38. See Chapter 9 Churchill *infra*.

39. Judgment of 28 November 1978, Series A, Vol.29.

40. See Golsong in Matscher/Petzold (Eds), n. 15 *supra* p. 241.

41. *Marckx* case n. 16 *supra* para. 58.

in Belgian law was prospective only and sought support for this view from the case law of the European Court of Justice.[42] Such a solution is possible, as is prospective overruling, but others may better reflect the local legal tradition. In fact, in view of the terms of Article 53 of the Convention, it is arguable that the consequences of a judgment of the Court within the domestic jurisdiction are questions of domestic, rather than Convention, law. In the United Kingdom a comparable issue is the long battle as to the effect of an unlawful piece of subordinate legislation or an unlawful administrative act has been resolved on the basis that the legislation or act is absolutely void.[43] One solution to mitigate the rigours of this rule is for the courts to retain a discretion to refuse a remedy by way of judicial review, *inter alia* if administrative chaos would result.[44] However, that discretionary technique is not provided for in the Convention or in the case law which interprets it.

These rigid factors seem to suggest a more fundamental effect for judgments of the Court, as does the character of the rights contained in the Convention themselves. On this view it would seem surprising that the authoritative interpretation of human rights and fundamental freedoms should be prospective from the (accidental) date when a judgment is given.

A third issue arising in an acute form from the review of legislation by reference to the Convention is the problem of the Court changing its mind. This difficulty arises from the criteria which the Court applies in evaluating the compliance of legislation with the Convention. The Court stated in *Marckx* that it

> could not but be struck by the fact that the domestic law of the great majority of the Member States of the Council of Europe has evolved and is continuing to evolve . . .[45]

The Court relies to some extent in interpreting the Convention on comparative material to evaluate the scope of the obligations imposed in different European jurisdictions. It is essential, if the Convention is to be a living instrument, that account should be taken of the evolution of national perceptions of basic rights.

42. *Defrenne v. Sabena*, ECR 1976, p.480.

43. *Anisminic v. Foreign Compensation Commission* [1969] 2 AC p.147 per Lord Reid and see Wade: Unlawful Administration Action (1967) 83 LQR 526 and (1968) 84 LQR 95.

44. *Dorset Yacht Co. Ltd. v. Home Office* [1970] AC 1004 per Lord Diplock.

45. *Marckx* case n. 16 *supra*, para. 41. See also similar considerations in the *Dudgeon* case n. 23 *supra*.

Nevertheless, judicial decision-making involves distinguishing between the wheat and the chaff and the protection of fundamental rights will inevitably involve more than establishing a 'European lowest common denominator'.

The difficulties of making this a clear distinction may be illustrated to some extent by the Court's attitude in the transsexual cases of *Rees*[46] and *Cossey*[47]. Both cases concerned the United Kingdom and the complaints of non-recognition for legal purposes of post-operative transsexuals' new sexual identities, and in the second case the applicant's right to marry.

The cases, which were lodged within five years of one another (1979 and 1984) and in which judgments were given within four years, relate to essentially the same legal circumstances. In *Rees* the Commission was of the unanimous opinion that Article 8 was violated. 'The failure of the United Kingdom to contemplate measures which would make it possible to take account in the applicant's civil status of the changes which [had] lawfully occurred [amounted] to a veritable failure to recognise the respect due to his private life'. They also held unanimously that there was no breach of Article 12 (the right to marry).[48]

The Court held there was no breach of Article 8 (12 votes to 3) but added a qualifying afterthought in the following terms:[49]

> The Court is conscious of the seriousness of the problems affecting these persons and the distress they suffer. The Convention has always to be interpreted and applied in the light of current circumstances. The need for appropriate legal measures should therefore be kept under review having regard particularly to scientific and societal developments.

The Court's judgment in *Cossey* contains a similar qualification to that cited from the *Rees* case above. The judgment is subject to a remarkable dissent by Judge Martens.

The difficulty which arises is to know *when* societal changes will have reached the point at which the Court will change its mind. As Judge Martens argues, a majority of Member States have in fact taken legislative steps to recognise a changed legal status for transsexuals. That was not enough, but what will be? Giving the instruction 'on your marks' to the legislature is not clearly one of the

46. Judgment of 17 October 1986, Series A, Vol. 106.
47. Judgment of 27 September 1990, Series A, Vol. 184.
48. Application No.9532/81 Rap.Comm. 12.12.84.
49. *Rees* case n. 46 *supra* para. 47.

tasks of the Court under Article 19 of the Convention.

Actual reversals of the Court's case law are rare but one has openly arisen in the *Borgers* case[50] which reversed the *Delcourt* case.[51] The cases concerned the Belgian practice whereby the *procureur général* made submissions to the Court of Cassation after the defendant's case has been closed and retired to attend the deliberations of the Court, without exercising a vote in those deliberations. In *Delcourt* a unanimous court found no violation of Article 6 of the Convention whereas in *Borgers* the Court found a systematic violation of this provision. The Court attempted to affirm its earlier reasoning in *Delcourt*[52] but the dissenting opinions of four judges[53] made the difficulties of the Court's change of view plain. Foremost amongst these is the problem of Belgium's legitimate reliance for twenty years on the finding in *Delcourt* that the national practice complied with Article 6 and the absence of convincing reasons for the Court's change of mind.

These issues illustrate some of the difficult technical questions to which the review of legislation gives rise.

III. THE REVIEW OF LEGISLATION IN DOMESTIC LAW

TURNING from these issues which relate to the *effect* of legislative review, consideration should be given briefly to the *means* whereby legislation is reviewed in domestic law.

The Member States of the Council of Europe may be divided into three categories in this respect. The first category provides for legislation to be tested by the courts for conformity with the constitution. The procedure for raising such a challenge is crucially important. In jurisdictions where this option is available, the legislation may be challenged as unconstitutional in the context of proceedings which relate to the application of that legislation. The ordinary court trying the question relating to the application of the legislation may refer the constitutional challenge to a specialist constitutional court.[54] The challenge relates to the

50. *Borgers* case judgment of 30 October 1991, Series A, Vol. 214.
51. *Delcourt* case judgment of 17 January 1970, Series A, Vol. 11.
52. *Borgers* case n. 51 *supra* para. 24.
53. *Ibid* pps. 35-38 and notably Judges Martens and Storme at pps.40-63.
54. This is in outline the position in Austria and Italy and represents one of the options for

legislation, rather than its application to the facts which has not yet been made. The *locus standi* for lodging such a challenge is provided by being a party to proceedings in which the impugned legislation is at issue and the availability of such a challenge is controlled by the decision of the trial court as to whether or not a legitimate constitutional challenge has been raised to the legislation. As a rule, where a constitutional reference is made, its effect is suspensive of the legal relations between the parties to the litigation, but difficult problems arise as to the effect of the constitutional proceedings on the validity of the legislation and on its effect on third parties.[55]

A number of jurisdictions are in the second category. They adopt a different approach to the control of legislative conformity with the constitution in providing for review of legislation before it comes into force or enactment, or within a short period thereafter. In Belgium the Commité de Concertation may consider this question.[56] In France the Conseil Constitutionnel plays a similar role[57] and this model has been emulated in Portugal. A similar possibility is provided in Ireland[58] and in the Federal Republic of Germany.

The third response to the question of the control of constitutional conformity of legislation is also widespread. It is to exclude such review. In the Netherlands,[59] Greece[60] and in Italy[61] the constitution prevents abstract review in terms. In France and Luxembourg the absence of any review of legislation reflects the doctrine of the separation of powers: legislation is the expression of the popular will through the legislature, and so is not a matter for the courts to evaluate.

This very short summary of the distinct types of constitutional review which operate in the domestic law of some European countries serves to underline the

constitutional review in the Federal Republic of Germany.

55. Thus the German Federal Constitutional Court may make an interim order under Article 93(1)GG suspending the operation of primary legislation while its conformity with the Basic Law is determined. An example is the National Census Act which was suspended during the proceedings which were brought to challenge it.

56. Article 32 Act on Institutional Reform 9 August 1988, as amended by Act of 16 June 1989.

57. Article 61 French Constitution.

58. Article 26 of the Constitution of Ireland.

59. Article 120 Constitution of the Netherlands.

60. Article 93 No. 4 Greek Constitution of 1975.

61. Article 134 Italian Constitution as interpreted.

importance of the jurisdiction which the Court and the Commission have developed to review legislation for conformity with the Convention.

Although various of the Member States of the Council of Europe allow individual constitutional complaints,[62] these are essentially different from the control of legislation. They allow a supreme or constitutional court to consider complaints that an individual's rights have been infringed by a particular decision or set of proceedings. These complaints are directly comparable with the individual complaints relating to specific individual circumstances under Article 25(1).[63]

The crucial distinction between the operation of these individual complaints and the constitutional control of legislation where it exists in domestic law is procedural. Whereas in individual complaints, review is open to an individual with direct access to the relevant court, both *locus standi* and the power to refer legislation for review is much more closely regulated. Thus where legislation may be referred for constitutional validation, the ordinary court usually has complete control as to whether a reference is made. Similarly, where prepromulgation review is provided for, those eligible to refer legislation for validation are usually members of the legislature or the President or equivalent constitutional figure.

IV. IMPLICATIONS FOR THE UNITED KINGDOM

THE traditional view of the United Kingdom constitution places it in the restrictive category where constitutional review is not provided by the courts. Parliament legislates. As Willes J put it, 'Acts of Parliament are the law of the land and we do not sit as a Court of Appeal from Parliament'.[64]

This is not quite true now, 120 years later. One court of justice in particular, the European Court of Justice, has confirmed that the courts may, and *must* review legislation for conformity with European Community law, as the

62. Such as those in Belgium to the Cour d'Arbitrage, by reference to Articles 6, 6 bis and 17 of the Constitution, the Verfassungsbeschwerde in the Federal Republic of Germany, proceedings for constitutional right in Ireland and the Recurso de Amparo in Spain.

63. See n. 9 and 10 *supra*.

64. *Lee v. Bude and Torrington Ry.* (1871) LR & CP 576.

Factortame case illustrates.[65]

In May 1989 the House of Lords ruled that, as a matter of domestic law, it had no jurisdiction to grant interim relief against the Crown, and so to suspend the operation of the Merchant Shipping Act 1988 which was alleged to be invalid to the extent that it prevented Community nationals, rather than British nationals, from owning fishing vessels fishing from the United Kingdom. The Court of Justice made an Order for interim measures and held that the pre-eminence of Community Law required the courts to be able to suspend and revoke legislation if its conformity with the EC Treaty was seriously in doubt.

The principle of legislative review is therefore established in our law. Since we are used to our constitution being amended by the courts, this change has not created undue difficulty – the position may very well be different for some of our Community partners, where the courts have not been given such a review power, or where it is significantly restricted.[66]

The *Factortame* case may be a pointer to more than merely a change – or revolution – in our constitution. It could provide an indication of the way in which the incorporation of the Convention, and the concomitant incorporation of the power to review legislation, might be achieved.

It is clear after *Brind*[67] that the English courts may not refer to the Convention except where the rules of statutory construction require it. Lord Bridge, for one, thought it impossible for the courts to incorporate the Convention substantively when Parliament had so obviously chosen to be satisfied with allowing the right of individual petition rather than legislating to incorporate.

However, the issue which was decided in *Factortame* was not whether the Treaty was superior law to English law, but whether a remedy should be provided to ensure that that rule was applied in an effective way. This approach is characteristic of the common lawyer's concern for remedies; at least for cases in Community law, *Factortame* swept away the procedural obstacle that historically interim relief could not be granted against the Crown.

It is not impossible that a similarly procedural approach to incorporation of the remedies provided under the Convention could be pursued. It would preserve the

65. *Factortame Ltd and others v. Secretary of State for Transport* Case 213/89 [1991] 1 All ER 70.

66. See n. 56-8 *supra*.

67. *Brind and others v. Secretary of State* [1991] 1 All ER 720, HL.

tradition that the English courts are unused to applying provisions such as the Convention, and are certainly not very familiar with reviewing legislation. As the short references to the position in some other domestic jurisdictions show, the Commission and the Court in Strasbourg have assumed a role in this respect which is denied to many national courts. Nevertheless the Court has shown itself alert to some of the special difficulties to which the review of legislation gives rise and the exercise of this jurisdiction has not been objected to by Member States, including the United Kingdom, which have no national experience of its exercise.

If the United Kingdom is to consider aspects of incorporation of the Convention, it could do worse than to protect, in domestic law, the remedy which applying to Strasbourg already provides. In the *Avon County Council* case[68] the Court of Appeal has shown a determination to stay the exercise of public power by the use of Order 53 rule 3(10)(a). Does principle prevent such a stay from applying until the determination of Strasbourg, rather than domestic, proceedings?

Obviously the slowness of Strasbourg proceedings is a major disincentive, but those proceedings can be accelerated[69] and a radical overhaul to streamline the Convention procedure is overdue and under discussion.[70] The review of legislation for conformity with the Convention is a particularly difficult task for any national court to undertake, in view of the importance of the consequences of the decision for third parties as well as the difficulty of applying the Convention in an area where no interpretation may yet have been given by the Court in Strasbourg.[71] There is a case for developing a special procedure for such cases, which could involve the domestic courts as a filter in a similar way to references to the European Court of Justice under Article 177 of the EC Treaty.[72]

68. *R v. Secretary of State for Education and Science, ex parte Avon County Council* [1991] 1 All ER 282.

69. In the *Soering* case judgment was given by the Court within a year of the application being lodged with the Commission.

70. The Committee of Ministers has established a Committee of Experts to report on reform of the Convention procedure.

71. For a more restrictive view of the Court's ability to undertake this legislative control, see Golsong *op cit* n. 40 *supra*.

72. This solution seems more practical than the well-rehearsed suggestion that a full EEC 177-style reference procedure should be introduced for individual complaints.

As *Factortame* underlines, it is not every case in which interim measures will be needed. It is true that the Rules of Procedure of both the Commission and the Court allow an indication of 'interim measures' to be given to the parties but its value has been more than questioned by the *Cruz Varas* case.[73] In keeping with the principle of the subsidiarity of the role of the Commission and the Court, it may be that the national judge, rather than the international tribunal, would be best placed to decide when such an important procedural remedy is needed.

73. Judgment of 20 March 1991, Series A, No. 201.

Chapter 9

ASPECTS OF COMPLIANCE WITH FINDINGS OF THE COMMITTEE OF MINISTERS AND JUDGMENTS OF THE COURT WITH REFERENCE TO THE UNITED KINGDOM

R.R. Churchill

I. INTRODUCTION

UNDER Articles 32(2) and 54 of the European Convention on Human Rights (hereafter referred to simply as the Convention) States which are parties are under an obligation to comply with decisions of the Committee of Ministers and the European Court of Human Rights finding them to be in breach of the Convention. For the effective functioning of the Convention it is obviously desirable, indeed essential, that this obligation should be fulfilled, especially in States (such as the United Kingdom) which have not incorporated the Convention into their domestic law, and in the light, too, of the weakness of the Convention's machinery for overseeing compliance with decisions of the Committee and Court.

The aim of this paper[1] is to consider whether and to what extent the United Kingdom has complied with decisions of the Committee and Court finding it to have violated the Convention, and to try to relate this question to the general theme of this book, the incorporation of the Convention into domestic law. As far as the first part of this aim is concerned, it is unfortunately not possible to

1. This paper is largely based on a much longer paper by the author and his colleague, James Young, "Compliance with Judgments of the European Court of Human Rights and Decisions of the Committee of Ministers: The Experience of the United Kingdom, 1975-87", which is published in Volume 62 of the British Year Book of International Law. The author is very grateful to Mr Young for allowing him to draw on this joint work and for preparing the bulk of the table at the end of this paper.

give a straightforward answer as to whether the United Kingdom has complied with decisions of the Committee and Court. The next section of this paper explains why this is so. This is followed by a consideration of the United Kingdom's record of compliance. For reasons of space only a brief overview of this record can be given, although a few cases will be discussed in detail to illustrate more general points relating to the subject of this paper and the theme of this book. The final part of the paper discusses whether incorporating the Convention would improve the United Kingdom's record of compliance.

II. SOME PRELIMINARY PROBLEMS

THIS section attempts to explain some of the problems involved in trying to answer the question of how far the United Kingdom has complied with decisions of the Committee and Court finding it to have violated the Convention. The main problem is that in most cases it is difficult to determine exactly the extent of the action which is necessary in order to comply with decisions of the Committee or Court. These bodies do not and cannot tell a State what action to take where it has been found to be in violation of the Convention. It is left to the State concerned to draw its own conclusions as to the action which ought to be taken.

Most cases under the Convention are brought by individuals and relate to the way in which the rights of a particular individual under the Convention may have been infringed. In a few such cases where a violation of the Convention is established, all that may be required for compliance is that some corrective administrative action be taken and/or compensation be paid. An example of such a case is *Gillow*,[2] where the Court found that Guernsey's housing laws were not in breach of the Convention but that the way in which they had been applied to Mr and Mrs Gillow was, and therefore ordered the payment of compensation. But in most cases the violation of an individual's rights is symptomatic of a more general defect in domestic law, so that compliance requires more than an individual remedy if further violations of the Convention are to be avoided. This is where the situation becomes more problematical.

As is the case with all judicial decisions, there may be problems in determining the precise *ratio* of a decision of the Court or Committee (and the decisions of the latter raise a particular problem as they are not reasoned).[3]

2. Series A No. 109 (1986).
3. While the Committee normally follows the opinion of the Commission as to whether there has

Given that a case relates to the circumstances of a particular individual, how far is it permissible to generalise from such circumstances? Or, in other words, at what level of abstraction can the decision be read? This problem can be illustrated by a fairly banal example. In the *Tyrer* case[4] the Court held that the birching of a 15-year old boy on the bare bottom as the penalty for commission of a criminal offence was 'degrading punishment' contrary to Article 3 of the Convention. From the language of the Court's judgment, it is clear that the *ratio* of this case is not simply that birching on the bare bottom is contrary to Article 3, but that all judicial birching of juveniles is contrary to Article 3. Probably one can go further and say that all judicial corporal punishment is contrary to Article 3, though whether one can go as far as to say that all corporal punishment is contrary to Article 3 is doubtful.

The above problems are compounded when the Court decides a case on fairly narrow grounds but nevertheless refers briefly to other issues which are wider. How far is it permissible to take the latter into account when assessing compliance? To some extent this is the same question of deciding how much effect ought to be given to the spirit as well as the letter of the Court's judgment. Again this problem may be illustrated by an example. In *Malone*,[5] the Court dealt with the case very largely in terms of whether there was sufficient legal authorisation of telephone tapping in the United Kingdom to meet the requirements of Article 8 of the Convention that this practice should be 'in accordance with the law'. Nevertheless, it also commented very briefly on the safeguards required if telephone tapping were also to meet the Convention's requirements of being 'necessary in a democratic society'. In assessing compliance in this case (which is discussed in more detail below), it is difficult to know whether much weight may legitimately be attached to these latter brief comments of the Court.

One consequence of the problems about assessing compliance just outlined is that it is quite possible for there to be genuine and legitimate differences of opinion about what is required in the way of compliance in many of the cases. It is important to bear this in mind when considering the account given of the United Kingdom's record of compliance in the next section of this paper.

been a violation of the Convention, it does not follow that the Committee thereby adopts all the reasoning of the Commission.

4. Series A No. 26 (1978); (1980) 2 EHRR 1.
5. Series A No. 82 (1984); (1985) 7 EHRR 14.

Before turning to this account, one further problem of assessing compliance in the case of the United Kingdom should be mentioned. The United Kingdom has separate legal systems for England and Wales, Scotland, and Northern Ireland, respectively, and has also extended the Convention to various dependent territories, including two such territories in Europe—the Channel Islands and the Isle of Man. The question thus arises as to whether, where the Convention has been violated in one jurisdiction, action to comply should also be taken in other jurisdictions where the law is the same. A full-hearted approach to compliance would suggest that it should.

III. AN OVERVIEW OF THE UNITED KINGDOM'S RECORD ON COMPLIANCE

UP TO the end of 1989 the United Kingdom had been found by the Court or Committee to have violated the Convention in 41 cases. For reasons of space it is obviously not possible to examine each of these cases in detail to see whether there has been compliance with decisions of the Court or Committee. Nevertheless, all the cases are summarised in the Table at the end of this paper, together with a brief account of and comment on the action taken by the United Kingdom to comply with the judgment of the Court or decision of the Committee. Based on this table and the study referred to in footnote 1, the following conclusions can be offered about the United Kingdom's record of compliance.

In 23 of the 41 cases there is not much doubt that the United Kingdom has complied (although in some cases compliance has not extended to reforming the law in dependent territories). These 23 cases include *inter alia* most of the decisions of the Committee of Ministers and the judgments of the Court in *Campbell and Cosans*,[6] *Ireland v. U.K.*,[7] *Weeks*,[8] *X*,[9] *Dudgeon*,[10] and *Young, James and Webster*.[11] In most of these cases compliance has involved the enactment of legislation. Compliance in most of these cases has been reasonably quick, usually within a year or so of the decision in question. Only in two

6. Series A No. 48 (1982); (1982) 4 EHRR 293.
7. Series A No. 25 (1978); (1980) 2 EHRR 25.
8. Series A No. 114 (1987); (1988) 10 EHRR 293.
9. Series A No. 46 (1981); (1982) 4 EHRR 188.
10. Series A No. 45 (1981); (1982) 4 EHRR 149.
11. Series A No. 44 (1980); (1982) 4 EHRR 38.

cases has compliance been excessively delayed—in *Campbell and Cosans*, where compliance came five years after the Court's judgment and was the result of a backbench amendment to a Government Bill carried against the Government's wishes, and *Weeks*, where compliance came four years after the judgment and was only prompted when the European Court's judgment in the subsequent case of *Thynne, Wilson and Gunnell*[12] showed the British Government's original view that *Weeks* was a unique case which did not require any general response by way of compliance, to have been mistaken.

In one case there has clearly not been compliance. This is *Tyrer*,[13] the Manx birching case, which was discussed briefly earlier. The Manx authorities have not amended the law which authorises the birching of juvenile offenders, nor have the United Kingdom authorities sought to impose legislation outlawing such birching, something which would be constitutionally possible, apparently for fear of offending Manx opinion on the issue. However, no birching of juvenile offenders appears to have occurred since the *Tyrer* case, and the Isle of Man High Court has ruled that Manx courts should not impose a sentence of birching unless other forms of punishment were unsuitable.[14]

In the remaining 17 cases it is debatable whether there has been compliance. These include *inter alia* the numerous prisoners cases, *Malone*,[15] *Brogan*,[16] *The Sunday Times*,[17] and the various Article 13 cases. Three of these—*Malone*, *Brogan* and the Article 13 cases—will be used as examples and examined in some detail in order to explain how the problems referred to in section II above arise in practice and how, therefore, it is possible for it to be debatable as to whether there has been compliance. These three examples have also been chosen because they help to illuminate the general theme of this book.

In *Malone* the Court found the then practice of telephone tapping in operation in the United Kingdom contrary to Article 8 of the Convention because it did not meet that article's requirement of being 'in accordance with the law'. This was because the law was not clear, in particular as to the way and circumstances in which the authorities could tap telephone calls. The United Kingdom's response

12. Series A No. 190 (1990).
13. Op. cit. in n. 4.
14. *Teare v. O'Callaghan* (1982) 4 EHRR 232.
15. Op. cit. in n. 5.
16. Series A No. 145 (1988); (1989) 11 EHRR 117.
17. Series A No. 30 (1979); (1980) 2 EHRR 245.

to the Court's judgment was the enactment of the Interception of Communications Act 1985. At first sight the Act appears to comply with the Court's judgment. The Act provides that a telephone may only be tapped, under a warrant issued by the Secretary of State, for one of the following purposes: (1) the interests of national security; (2) for the purpose of preventing or detecting serious crime; or (3) for the purpose of safeguarding the economic well-being of the United Kingdom. Superficially each of these grounds seems reasonably clear. Further examination, however, suggests the opposite. Taking the first purpose, national security: in debates on the Bill the Government defined national security as 'concerned with espionage, terrorism and subversion and also with the acquisition of intelligence in support of the Government's defence and overseas policies'.[18] While the first half of this definition seems reasonably clear, it must be doubted whether the second half is sufficiently precise to meet the requirements of the Convention. Turning to the next purpose, preventing or detecting serious crime, 'serious crime' is defined in section 10(3) of the Act. Again, while much of the definition is acceptably clear, there are some elements which are very vague and which seem insufficiently precise to meet the requirements of the Convention. Thus, 'serious crime' includes offences which result in 'substantial financial gain' (substantial by what criteria?) and offences involving 'conduct by a large number of persons in pursuit of a common purpose'. The final purpose, safeguarding the economic well-being of the United Kingdom, is again vague (though admittedly it is one of the grounds on which interferences with communications are permitted under paragraph 2 of Article 8). Of this purpose the Government said that it is 'concerned with interception that is necessary for the effective protection of the country's economic interests at the international level', although the Government spokesman, Lord Whitelaw, felt unable to give even hypothetical examples of what this might cover because to do so would in itself be damaging.[19]

In its judgment in *Malone* the Court did not find it necessary to consider the requirement that, to be valid under the Convention, telephone tapping must be 'necessary in a democratic society'. However, the Court did comment, referring to its earlier judgment in *Klass v. Federal Republic of Germany*,[20] that an acceptable system of telephone tapping must contain 'adequate guarantees against

18. H.L. Deb., May 16, 1985, Vol. 463, col. 1257.
19. H.L. Deb., June 6, 1985, Vol. 464, col. 879.
20. Series A No. 28 (1978); (1980) 2 EHRR 214.

abuse'.[21] There must be serious doubts as to whether the Interception of Communications Act does provide such guarantees. The main potential guarantee is the Tribunal set up by the Act to investigate complaints of telephone tapping. There are a number of features about its role and powers which cast doubt on its adequacy as a guarantee against abuse. First, if the Tribunal finds there was an interception which was not authorised by a warrant it cannot investigate further or inform the complainant of this fact: presumably it is intended that the Tribunal should inform the police (since prima facie an offence has been committed), but the Act does not require it to do so. Secondly, where tapping has been done under a warrant, the Tribunal can review the legality of its exercise only on the principles of judicial review. This may be too narrow to provide an effective safeguard against abuse. Thirdly, if a person's telephone has been legally tapped, he cannot be told this. All he can be told is that there has been no breach of ss.2-5. From this he might deduce that his telephone has been lawfully tapped. Equally valid deductions would be that his telephone has been tapped but not under warrant; that his telephone has not been tapped at all; or that the Tribunal has been unable to discover what has happened. A final defect with the Tribunal is that its decisions are not reviewable in the courts.

In addition, other aspects of the Act cast doubt as to whether it offers sufficient guarantees against abuse. These include the rules on exclusion of evidence in s.9 which would make it impossible for an individual to bring civil proceedings against a Minister or anyone else based on breach of the Act. Nor could an individual bring a private prosecution, because under the Act the consent of the DPP is necessary.

All in all, the safeguards provided by the Act compare very unfavourably with those that exist in Germany which were at issue in the *Klass* case. Given what the Court said in that case, it must be very doubtful whether the British safeguards meet the requirements of the Convention. One might add, too, that the weakness of the British safeguards is compounded by the fact that the Convention has not been incorporated into British domestic law, so that it is impossible to bring an action before the British courts alleging that telephone tapping, whether or not authorised under the Act, has not been carried out in conformity with the requirements of the Convention.

A second example of a case where it is doubtful whether the United Kingdom has complied with the judgment of the Court is *Brogan*. In this case the Court

21. Para. 81 of the Court's judgment in *Malone*.

found that the holding of Brogan and his fellow applicants under the Prevention of Terrorism Act (under which those suspected of terrorist offences may be held without being charged for a maximum of seven days) for periods ranging from four days and six hours to six days and sixteen hours was a breach of Article 5(3) of the Convention, under which anyone arrested on suspicion of having committed a crime must be brought 'promptly' before a judge. The British Government's response to the judgment was not, as one might perhaps have expected, to amend the Prevention of Terrorism Act to require those suspected of terrorist offences to be brought before a judge within some period of less than four days after first being detained. Instead, rather than amend the Act, the Government made a derogation under Article 15 of the Convention. This raises two questions. First, whether there is in the United Kingdom (especially in Great Britain, as opposed to Northern Ireland) a 'public emergency threatening the life of the nation', which is required in order for a State to avail itself of Article 15. Secondly, even if there is, whether the 'exigencies of the situation' 'strictly require' such a derogation from Article 5(3). It is doubtful whether the answers to these two questions are in the affirmative. However, any prolonged speculation on these two questions is unnecessary, as they are likely to be resolved in due course by the Convention organs. Recently the Commission has declared a number of applications admissible which challenge the legitimacy under the Convention of the United Kingdom's derogation.[22] It may also be added that the non-incorporation of the Convention has prevented such a challenge being mounted before British courts.

A final example of where it is doubtful whether the United Kingdom has complied with decisions of the Court and Committee is the series of cases where the United Kingdom has been found to be in breach of Article 13. As a prelude to discussing these cases, a few words must be said about the general problems of interpretation and application to which Article 13 has given rise. The article provides that 'everyone whose rights and freedoms as set forth in this Convention are violated shall have an effective remedy before a national authority'. This article is one of the more obscurely drafted provisions of the Convention and the views of the Convention organs as to its meaning have varied significantly since the Convention was adopted. Before 1978 the approach of the Commission, where a violation of Article 13 was alleged because the applicant had no effective

22. The European Court gave judgment upholding the effectiveness of the derogation in the *Brannigan and McBride* case on 26 May 1993.

remedy in domestic law for an alleged violation of one of the Convention's rights, was to ask whether the Convention right in question had in fact been violated. If it had, a violation of the Convention had been established without it being necessary to consider Article 13. If the Convention right had not been violated, then Article 13 did not apply. Under this approach Article 13 was largely tautologous. A major change of approach came in 1978 with the Court's judgment in the *Klass* case,[23] where the Court for the first time considered Article 13 in detail. The Court observed that it was not a pre-requisite for the application of Article 13 that some other Convention right had in fact been violated. What Article 13 required was that 'where an individual considers himself to have been prejudiced by a measure allegedly in breach of the Convention he should have a remedy before a national authority in order both to have his claim decided and, if appropriate, to obtain redress'.[24] This view of Article 13 has been followed by both the Court and Commission since the *Klass* case.

The United Kingdom has been found to have been in breach of Article 13 in five cases - three of the prisoners' correspondence cases (*Silver*,[25] *Campbell and Fell*,[26] and *Farrant*[27]), *Abdulaziz, Cabales and Balkandali*[28] and *Warwick*.[29] In each of these cases the British Government has taken the view that once it has remedied the other breaches of the Convention found by the Court or Committee in these cases, there is no longer a breach of Article 13 and therefore no further action need be taken. This is obviously a pre-*Klass* approach to Article 13. While it goes against the general approach of the Court and Commission to Article 13 since *Klass*, it must be conceded that there are passages in the Court's judgments in each of the cases concerned which hark back to the pre-*Klass* position and which would therefore justify the British Government's view that no specific action is required to remedy a breach of Article 13, however much this may be contrary to the general spirit of the Court's view of Article 13.

Each of the cases where it is doubtful whether there has been compliance, or compliance has been at best minimal has, of course, its own explanation for this

23. Op. cit. in n. 20.
24. Para. 64 of the Court's judgment.
25. Series A No. 63 (1983); (1983) 5 EHRR 347.
26. Series A No. 80 (1984); (1985) 7 EHRR 165.
27. Committee Res. DH (87) 3.
28. Series A No. 94 (1985); (1985) 7 EHRR 471.
29. Committee Res. DH (89) 5.

state of affairs. Nevertheless, some general reasons can be offered to explain why in some of the cases compliance has been less than full-hearted. Some of the cases—such as those concerning prisoners, telephone tapping, and, to a degree, immigration—involve areas where there has traditionally been a high degree of executive discretion in the United Kingdom, with only limited outside review. Clearly, successive British Governments have not wished to change this state of affairs more than the minimum necessary following rulings of the Convention organs. Some cases, such as *Brogan* and telephone tapping, have involved security issues, where again only minimum change is likely to be made. Finally, full-hearted compliance with the Article 13 cases could only be secured by incorporating the Convention—something to which successive British Governments, of whatever political hue, have consistently been opposed.

V. WOULD INCORPORATING THE CONVENTION IMPROVE COMPLIANCE?

As has been seen, the United Kingdom's record in complying with decisions of the Committee and Court finding it to have violated the Convention is rather patchy. In the light of the general theme of this book, it may be of interest to end this paper by speculating whether incorporating the Convention would improve the United Kingdom's record of compliance.

First of all, if the Convention were incorporated, there might well be fewer cases to be decided by the Convention organs, because some cases would have been settled before the British courts. Thus, there would be fewer decisions of the Court and Committee with which compliance would be necessary. This, however, would depend at least in part on the attitude of British judges when applying the Convention. Were they to take a narrow view of the Convention, then there could well be as many cases going to Strasbourg as before. In any case, as Dr. Kruger's paper shows, there is in fact no necessary correlation between the number of cases brought against a particular Contracting State and the status of the Convention in its domestic law.

If the Convention were incorporated, it would offer a new means for putting pressure on the Government to take action to comply with a judgment of the Court or a decision of the Committee of Ministers where it appeared to be slow or reluctant to do so. In such a situation an action could be brought before a British court, possibly by the original applicant but more likely by another person, alleging a continuing breach of the Convention (as, for example, Thynne, Wilson and Gunnell might have done after the failure of the Government to reform the law following the European Court's judgment in *Weeks*, rather than having to bring a case before the Convention organs). A decision by a British court upholding such an allegation would obviously put pressure on the Government to take action to comply.

Such a decision might even go further, depending on the status of the Convention in British law following incorporation. If the Convention were to prevail over inconsistent legislation, then the decision of the British court might, in some circumstances, have the effect of achieving compliance. An illustration of how this could happen can be seen from an example from the Netherlands, where the Convention is superior to domestic legislation. In the *Winterwerp* case[30] the Dutch Lunacy Act of 1884 was found by the European Court to be contrary to the Convention. In spite of various Bills to amend the Act being published and presented to the Dutch Parliament, none has (or at least until recently, had) been passed, with the result that the 1884 Act remains formally in force. However, as a result of various decisions of the Dutch Supreme Court in the early 1980s, the offending sections of the 1884 Act have been set aside.

While incorporating the Convention into British law would be unlikely to make a major impact in improving the United Kingdom's record of complying with decisions of the Court and Committee finding it to have violated the Convention, it is likely that it would nevertheless lead to some improvement in this matter.

V. CONCLUSIONS

IN the early part of this paper it was pointed out that one of the problems in carrying out a study of how far any particular Contracting State to the European Convention on Human Rights has complied with decisions of the Court and Committee finding it to have violated the Convention is the fact that it is difficult in many cases to determine exactly what action ought to be taken in order for there to be full-hearted compliance with such decisions. Neverthless, in spite of this problem, it is reasonable to conclude that in the case of the United Kingdom its record of compliance falls some way short of the ideal. There are various reasons why compliance has been less than total, but only in one instance - the Article 13 cases - is the non-incorporation of the Convention a major factor in the failure to comply. Nevertheless, if the Convention were incorporated, it is likely that there would be some improvement in the United Kingdom's record of compliance generally, and not just in those cases involving Article 13.

30. Series A No. 33 (1979); (1980) 2 EHRR 387.

TABLE SHOWING CASES WHERE THE UNITED KINGDOM HAS BEEN FOUND TO HAVE VIOLATED THE CONVENTION AND THE UNITED KINGDOM'S RESPONSE, 1975-1989

Case	Article	UK Response	Comments
Ireland (Court 18.1.78) (treatment of detainees during interrogation)	3	Administrative action in form of formal renunciation of 'five techniques' Directives to security forces forbidding assaults on detainees. Change in medical procedures. New complaints investigation procedures	Action taken in advance of Court judgment. But some practices continued, probably in breach of Convention. Further measures in 1980 following Bennett Committee Report enough to comply
Tyrer (Court 25.4.78) (corporal punishment in the Isle of Man)	3	Letter to Lieutenant Governor informing him that Manx law in breach of the Convention	No change in law. Corporal punishment still theoretically possible, but no instance since *Tyrer*
Soering (Court 7.7.89) (extradition to USA where risk of being subject to 'death row' phenomenon)	3	Soering extradited to USA on condition that he would not be tried on any charges for which penalty was death	Action contrary to literal reading in Court's judgment (which assumed that if Soering were extradited, he would be subject to possible death penalty), but conforms to its spirit
Brogan (Court 29.11.88) (excessively long detention of suspected terrorists before being brought before a judge)	5(3)	Derogation made under Article 15	Questionable whether derogation accords with requirements of Article 15. Currently being challenged before Convention organs

Case	Article	UK Response	Comments
X (Court 5.11.81) (failure to provide means of review of indefinite detention of mental patient)	5(4)	Mental Health (Amendment) Act 1982, s.28(4) and Sch.1. In Northern Ireland Mental Health (NI) Order 1986, SI 1986 No.595, Part V. For Scotland see *Gordon* below.	Compliance adequate, effective 2 years after judgment
B (Committee 22.4.83) (as *X* above)	5(4)	No further action in light of *X*	
C, Medway & Ball (Committee 25.1.85) as *X* above)	5(4)	As *B*	
Gordon (Committee 9.9.86) (failure as in *X* but under Scottish law)	5(4)	Mental Health (Amendment) (Scotland) Act 1983 s.21	Compliance as in England and Wales in *X*
Zamir (Committee 25.1.85) (delay in deportee's *habeas corpus* application)	5(4)	Revision of Rules of Supreme Court	Delay due to failure by various administrative authorities. Claimed compliance not relevant. Failure of procedure, rather than system, put UK in breach
Weeks (Court 2.3.87) (failure to provide means of review of detention of discretionary life prisoner)	5(4)	*Weeks* pardoned, compensation paid. No general reform of the law until Criminal Justice Act 1991	UK's claim that *Weeks'* case unique so no general reform of the law required, shown to be wrong by *Thynne, Wilson and Gunnell*
Golder (Court 21.2.75) (prisoner's access to legal advice re treatment in prison)	6(1) and 8	Access permitted after exhaustion of internal complaints procedure ('prior ventilation rule')	Inadequate compliance failing to take account of Court's reasoning
Kiss (Committee 19.4.78 (as *Golder*)	6(1)	Reform already carried out as a result of *Golder*	For doubts as to compliance, see *Golder*
Hilton (Committee 24.4.79) (as *Golder*)	6(1)	As *Kiss*	As *Kiss*

Case	Article	UK Response	Comments
Campbell & Fell (Court 28.6.84) (prior ventilation rule and prisoner's access to legal advice)	6(1) and 8	Rule already abolished (see *Silver* below)	
(lack of confidentiality in prisoner's conference with lawyer)	6(1)	Change in Prison Standing Orders in 1981	Anticipatory compliance during reform of Orders after *Silver*
(publication of prison disciplinary decision)	6(1)	Letter to chairmen of Boards of Visitors 12.7.84, followed by amendment of *Manual on Conduct of Adjudications in Prison*	Adequate and prompt compliance
(right to legal advice and representation in prison disciplinary proceedings)	6(3)(b) (c)		Doubtful if circumstances in which legal representation allowed in accordance with judgment
(no effective national remedy	13	No action taken. UK Government view that remedial action under other Articles breached is enough	UK probably remains in breach, on better view of Article 13
Silver (Court 25.3.83) (restrictions on prisoners' correspondence, some unpublished)	6(1) and 8	Revised Prison Standing Order 5, into force December 1981. Simultaneous ventilation rule replaced prior ventilation rules re correspondence with legal adviser (see *Golder* above). Restrictions on content and correspondents eased. Standing Order published	In general anticipatory compliance taken pending case which appears adequate, but doubts as to whether some remaining restrictions on correspondence are compatible with Article 8
(no effective national remedy)	13	No action taken (see *Campbell and Fell*)	
Brady et al (Committee 27.6.86) (censorship of correspondence and access to legal advice)	6(1) and 8	Reform as a result of *Silver* already carried out	In this and the following four Committee decisions the UK thought that no response was necessary. For doubts as to compliance see *Silver*
Marritt et al (Committee 27.8.86) (as *Brady* above)	6(1) and 8	As *Brady*	
Jenkinson et al (Committee 19.9.86) (as *Brady* above)	6(1) and 8	As *Brady*	

Case	Article	UK Response	Comments
Farrant et al (Committee 12.2.87) (as *Brady*, and prisoner's right to prosecute privately)	6 and 8	As *Brady*, but also abolition of bar on private prosecutions	Change in private prosecutions result of *Raymond v. Honey* [1983] 1 AC 1
(lack of effective national remedy)	13	As *Campbell & Fell* above	
Byrne et al (Committee 20.3.87) (as *Brady*, but also challenge to simultaneous ventilation rule)	6(1) and 8	As *Silver*, and abolition of simultaneous ventilation rule	Abolition of simultaneous ventilation rule a result of *ex p Anderson* [1984] QB 778
Grace (Committee 19.9.89) (prisoners' correspondence)	8	As *Byrne*	
Boyle and Rice (Court 27.4.88) (prisoners' correspondence)	8	Violation a result of erroneous application of Prison Rules. Measures taken to ensure Rules are correctly applied in future	
Orchin (Committee 27.10.83) (delays in criminal procedure)	6(1)	Administrative directives to reduce delays	Prompt compliance appears adequate
McVeigh, O'Neill & Evans (Committee 24.3.82) (right to contact spouse after lawful detention)	8	Criminal Law Act 1977, s.62. Equivalent provisions subsequently introduced in Scotland in 1980, in Northern Ireland in 1987	Anticipatory compliance by backbench initiative
Dudgeon (Court 22.10.81) (homosexuality law in Northern Ireland)	8	Homosexual Offences (Northern Ireland) Order 1982 (in force 9.12.82) decriminalising private homosexual acts between consenting adults	Brought Northern Ireland law into line with England & Wales and Scotland. UK still in breach as regards Isle of Man and Jersey
Malone (Court 2.8.84) (telephone tapping and metering)	8	Interception of Communications Act 1985 (in force 10.4.86). Established machinery to regulate and monitor telephone and metering	Compliance at best minimal. System of regulation imprecise in grounds on which tapping and metering permitted. Inadequate safeguards against abuse

Case	Article	UK Response	Comments
Abdulaziz, Cabales & Balkandali (Court 28.5.85) (sex discrimination in immigration rules regarding spouses)	8, 13 and 14	Immigration Rules amended August 1985. Further discrimination removed by Immigration Act 1988 s.1 and Immigration Rules 1989. Article 13, no response beyond above (see *Campbell & Fell* above)	Immediate response adequate for persons in applicants' position. Further measures re certain Commonwealth citizens 1988 and re business people 1989. Compliance still apparently necessary for students
Gillow (Court 24.11.86) (refusal of licence to live on Guernsey)	8	Compensation to applicants	Adequate compliance since breach was unacceptable application of acceptable principles
B, R and *W* (Court 8.7.87) (procedures concerning parental access to children in local authority care)	6(1)	S.34 of Children Act 1989 (in force October 1991) provides for all questions concerning parental contact with children in local authority care to be determinable by a court	Partial anticipatory compliance in 1983 amendments to Child Care Act 1980. Complete compliance effective four years after Court's judgment
	8	S.22 of Act provides for greater parental involvement in local authority decision-making	
O (Court 8.7.87) (as *B, R* and *W*)	6(1)	As *B, R* and *W*	
H (Court 8.7.87) (as *B, R* and *W*, plus delay in Court proceedings re access and adoption)	6(1) and 8	No action appears to have been taken	Delay due to tardiness of local authority in filing evidence. Therefore no general reform of the law necessary
Gaskin (Court 7.7.89) (access of person in local authority care to personal files held by authority)	8	No action appears (yet) to have been taken	

Case	Article	UK Response	Comments
Sunday Times (Court 26.4.79) (injunction preventing publication of article)	10	Contempt of Court Act 1981	Delay due to inclusion of response in more general reform of contempt law. Doubt as to adequacy since much left for judicial interpretation
T (Committee 4.12.86) (prisoner's access to reading and writing materials)	10	Revision of Standing Order 4.5.85	Adequate compliance anticipating Committee's decision. Similar changes in Northern Ireland and Scotland
Young, James & Webster (Court 13.8.81) (trade union closed shop)	11	Employment Act 1980	Anticipatory compliance. Court's ruling was in accordance with UK Government's policies. Subsequent legislation proof against breach of Article 11 as regards closed shop
Hamer (Committee 2.4.81) (right of prisoner serving fixed term of imprisonment to marry while serving term)	12	Change of administrative practice to allow temporary release for such prisoners to marry in 1977	Response failed to take life prisoners into account
Draper (Committee 2.4.81) (right of prisoner serving life imprisonment to marry)	12	Facilities offered to Draper to marry. Marriage Act 1983 (in force 1.5.84) allowing prisoners to be married in prison	Full compliance 3 years after Committee's decision. Right also given to long-stay mental patients to marry in hospital
Campbell & Cosans (Court 25.2.82) (corporal punishment in Scottish State schools)	Protocol 1, Art.2	Education (No.2) Act 1986, ss.47 and 48, Education (Corporal Punishment) (Northern Ireland) Order 1987	Complete compliance for State sector, 5 year delay. Ultimately compliance result of back-bench initiative
Warwick (Committee 2.3.89) (corporal punishment in English state school)	Protocol 1, Art.2	Compliance already achieved. See *Campbell & Cosans*	
(lack of effective national remedy)	13	No further action taken (see *Campbell & Fell* above)	